Symbols and Parables

Symbols and Parables

Dr Alok Pandey

Title: Symbols and Parables
Author: Dr Alok Pandey

ISBN: 978-93-92209-37-6
Edition: I

Published by:
BluOne India LLP

Publisher's Address:
306, Tower-I, Assotech Business Cresterra,
Plot No. 22, Sector 135, Noida.

Website: www.bluone.ink
Email: publisher@bluone.ink

Copyright © 2023 Dr Alok Pandey
All rights reserved.

Cover design by Geetanjali Ahooja

Printed in India

*This book is offered to Sri Aurobindo and the Mother whose light has revealed many profound truths of the past while opening the doors to the future.
This work is the result of their vision applied to these parables and stories*

Contents

Preface ix

Part One: Parables of Light

Prayers	3
Guru	5
That Thou Art, Tat Tvam Asi	7
The Sea	9
The Two Gospels of Prahlad and Hiranyakashyap	12
The Flute Player	16
Ravana, the Fall from Grace	19
The Great Flood	22
The Test of Fire	29
Sri Krishna and the Seven Seers	31
Ways of Nature	34
The Journey: The Fable of the two Paths	36

Part Two: In the Master's Light

Love	61
Truth	63
Sowing the Seed	67
How Many Paths	70
What Humanity Really Needs	72
The Birth and Death of Suffering and Sin	77

The Egg and the Chick	80
The Nectar of Immortality	83
The Dwarf with Three Strides	92
The Soul's Dwelling Place	100
Ways of the Master	105
Karna, the Fallen Great	107
Adhikara Bheda	112
The Second Coming	116

Preface

India is a land of stories that are woven in the fabric of its life. These stories have cultivated the mind of the race giving birth to new and creative ideas. They have nourished the deeper psychic and higher spiritual impulsions. They have played a great role in shaping and moulding the character of the people who dwelt in this wonderland that we know today as India. Beyond fact and fiction these stories build for us a complete view of a multi-layered Reality and provide us with a perception of life that looks deep behind appearances for the vision of Truth.

The stories in this book are written with the purpose of awakening us to this deeper vision that can bridge the gap between our surface views and the deeper truths they represent and provide us with a vision of reality that is often missed by the sensory mind involved with the appearances of events and circumstances.

The stories have been divided into two sections. Both sections contain a mix of known stories from Indian mythologies as well as new ones that have been used to convey a truth in the form of a fable. The difference, however, is in the format for the two sections. The first part is written in the usual story format while the second is in the form of a dialogue between seekers and the Master using the question-answer format. Each carries its own unique flavour and is laced with the dew drops of truth-light as received by the author during his passage of life and his dwelling deep into the tales that have enriched the human mind with deeper psychic and spiritual truths.

It is hoped that they will awaken a response in the same depths of the readers from where they have emerged in the author and help us grow towards the Light and the Right.

Part One
Parables of Light

Prayer

Prayers are like birds that climb from the earth to rise to the sky. But some are weak and stay near the ground. Others climb very high and travel far and wide to the distant lands of Light and Truth.

Some prayers are like parrots. They are simply learnt and mechanically repeated without their meaning stirring the depths of our souls. They look neat and nice but stop at that. They cannot fly far nor reach high. Some are like the crow, restless and doubting, full of fear and suspicion. They arise from our petty surface desires for this or that small object of life. These prayers have neither strength nor trust. They too do not reach high or far but sometimes they do get fulfilled due to sheer persistence with which they are done since nature rewards every effort that involves perseverance.

Others are like the pigeon and the dove. They are not strong but full of peace, born of trust. Hence, they call forth the bounty of nature for the fulfilment of what they seek. Yet others are like the eagle. They are precise and clear about their object and strong in their spirit of seeking. They rise high and far on the wings of concentration and arrive at their object swiftly. Even though they climb high, their object is low, the fulfilment of some earthly desire.

Rare are the prayers like the swan. Pure and clear, they ask for nothing but the very nectar of the gods. They reach farthest to distant horizons, far above the clouds, to the very abode of Shiva, the great god Ashutosh, the dispenser of all boons.

But the rarest of all is the prayer that resembles the phoenix. Such a prayer arises once in a thousand years.

Paradoxically it descends from the heavens and enters the bosom of the earth stirring it with sublime impulses. It is the prayer that the avatara does for the earth and mankind. Such are the prayers of the Mother for the earth as recorded in Her book, Prayers and Meditations.

Guru

Guru is the dispenser of light. Just as there are several sources of light so also are there several types of gurus. There are those unconnected with the earth like distant constellations or stars. They point the path to us that we may follow but neither give light nor warmth. Others are like the moon, close to the earth yet not intimately linked to its life. They shed light and shower the coolness of their grace in the human night. They show the way of escape out of the human night of ignorance to the silent heart of endless Space.

Yet others are like fire that give us warmth and comfort. They light up aspiration in our hearts and protect us from the lower impulses such as those of greed, fear, anger. They are like brief visitations of heavenly light clothed in forms more familiar to us. Of course, many pseudo gurus thrive on borrowed and artificial light like that of bulbs and tubes. They too serve a purpose in God's plan to make the night a little more bearable.

But seldom does one find the guru as the sun, the Divine avatara, shedding His light upon earth. He not only sheds Light but changes the seasons and the flow of time. He sustains and supports the transitions from one age to another and the evolutionary journey of life upon earth by His mere Presence. Not many can bear His closeness and the intense pressure of Heat and Light. Hardly can anyone even gaze at him except when he chooses to eclipse himself with a human cloak. All feel His warmth, share his Light and benefit from His power and splendour. Nothing is hidden from his sight and He knows all paths and every law since they originate from him. But none knows Him or can reach Him. Such a Master is born once in a thousand years or even less often. Such is our Lord and Master, Sri Aurobindo, whose mere Presence is enough to change the earthly season, who shines deathless in the eastern horizon revealing Time's secrets to earth and mankind.

That Thou Art, Tat Tvam Asi

A moth reached a congregation of fire lamps that had been lit atop a hill. As it neared the top, it met some fireflies glowing in the darkness below. The moth being an inquisitive one asked the firefly if it had ever seen the sun. Like the moth, the firefly grew blind in the day and therefore, knew not of it. But with an air of superior wisdom, it declared that there was no sun since it had never seen it. Perhaps, the sun was simply a tale told by some to create fear in others. For if there was one then why should not the firefly and the moth see it when they could very well see in the darkness and even light it with its flares. Little did it realise that its eyes, endowed to see in the dark and accustomed only to the night, cannot see the blazing light that comes up every day. And what to the moth and the firefly is a night is to the earth at large the light of day.

The moth proceeded further and as it came very close to the fire lamps it met a few sparks that flew out of the flames by the action of the winds. The moth repeated the question, "Is there a sun?" And the sparks in all humility replied, "We know not of that, but we do know from where we came. It is those flames that you see out there. Perhaps, they may know." So saying they vanished as suddenly as they had appeared. Soon, guided by the sparks, the moth reached the hilltop and stood close to the little lamps. One nearest to it was a small little flame that did not burn long enough to endure the night and glimpse the day. The moth repeated its question. The flame replied with superior wisdom, "The sun I have seen not. I know only the stars and the moon. Perhaps, it is this that they call sun or maybe the sun is simply a myth, a kind of super-flame much like me, a little bigger perhaps as I may be one day."

One nearer to it that had felt the dawn but seen not the sun responded more hopefully, "I think there is something called the sun because I have felt its light and warmth spread magically over the earth. But soon after the rare glimpse, I fainted and faded till some unseen hand lit me again tonight. But I think there is a sun since I have felt its glory and its touch. Maybe none can see it or know of it, yet one can feel it and sense it."

All this while there stood amidst them a flame, erect and silent like a concentrated mass of energy and force. When the moth approached it, the fire spoke not for a while. But seeing the moth's insistence and the flames around it stand in silent expectation, it addressed the whole group thus, "Yes, I have looked upon the sun since the fuel in me could withstand the burden of the long night as all who can thus endure with faith can see. But I have learnt another secret, that what burns in the sun also burns in me, that the sun and the fire are the same, one in essence, two in appearance." Thus, saying these deep words pregnant with Truth born of experience, the fire was quiet again. The little flames around lifted their arms in adoration and worship to the great fire that had revealed this great secret to them. But the moth felt an irresistible urge to jump and lose itself into the fire and thus, lose itself to find the sun by seeing through the eyes of the fire. For only they who are willing to lose their self, find the Self. Only those who die to the self of the ego, find the Divine self. And as the moth leapt into the great fire, one more spark jumped upward into the sky and the night began to recede as the glow lit the sky on the east.

The Sea

A group of young and old had gathered ashore. They had never seen the sea before, only read and heard about it. Soon a discussion followed. One who had neither read nor heard much simply exclaimed at the marvellous sight before him, "Wow! What a vast expanse of water. Who can ever measure it?"

Another who was well-versed with books on sea rushed to impress by his erudition, "Oh, you seem to be quite ignorant. Actually, quite a few have ventured but two among these, truly bravest among them tried to sail across the entire sea. Of these only one returned after ten long years. And of the other, one knows not the fate whether he was drowned or drifted to some friendly or hostile isle."

Surprised by his knowledge one turned to ask, "Is it true that the sea has many riches in its store?"

"I don't know exactly what riches the sea has," replied another eager to join the conversation and contribute his bit as well, "but I have heard through the word of mouth that there are some rare jewels in its depths."

"And some dangerous creatures as well," said another unable to resist, "the kind of which we do not see on land or near the shores."

And the knowledgeable man again, "Oh, he is talking of sharks and whales."

"And mermaids too," said one who was simple and full of wonder among them. And he added with a solemn religious tone, "and these mermaids can grant you boons of many kinds, pearls and riches if you would pray to them." A knowledgeable scientist whose scientific books had not mentioned anything about mermaids and boons strongly ridiculed these stories as fiction and imagination.

Soon the group of men divided into two camps. One was with the scientist and argued against the mermaids and boons. The other was with the simple credulous man who joined him even to pray to the mermaids for these treasures. This religious man had learnt a few incantations from his grandfather written in some sacred text thousands of years old. His grandfather who had never seen a mermaid or even the sea and died penniless had learnt this formula from his great grandfather who had learnt from his great grandfather and so on and so forth.

While all this was going on, a third group broke away from both and tried to philosophically reason out about the sea and its various possibilities. These again divided into several sects and sub-sects, some argued that the sea had nothing in its depths since they could see nothing, neither whales and sharks nor mermaids and pearls. They felt these speculations was a waste of time. All that the sea has are some fishes and turtles and all that one can know and needs to know is how to ply a boat on the waves and how to cast a net to catch the fish, crabs and prawns.

Others ridiculed the shallowness of this group who could see nothing beyond the tip of their nose and immediate utility. Still, others simply said, "Let's stop arguing and just enjoy this lovely sight and the beautiful sunrise." All, however, agreed on one thing that none knows fully about the sea and none can ever know. They even doubted if the story of the lone sailor crossing the sea itself was not a hoax. Yet none would venture to find out lest they met the unknown fate of the other sailor.

A known insecurity is better than an unknown certainty, they thought.

And as they thus debated and discussed, some tired and weary of the stories and philosophy of theories and dogmas of proofs and doubts of arguments and counterarguments of joy and the wonder and fear of the dangerous waves slept off. The others too followed these to the world of dreams with familiar lands and faces of love. Some dreamt of the roaring sea and the storms that sweep the surface. Others dreamt of unknown far-off isles inhabited by strange and unknown people.

But one youth among them kept awake. Unknown to others he was building a boat the whole night. And when the sun rose and there was daybreak once again, nothing had changed in the life of these men except for him who was young in spirit. Unseen to the eyes of those left behind on the shore he had sailed off to the delight of danger with faith and courage as his companions. They saw him not again and pondered over his fate. But the youth had gone far into the deep, gathering pearls, taming the waves, plumbing the depths, and braving the storms, with the lightning stars as his guide. When the winds blew softly, he conversed with mermaids who informed him to keep clean off the dangerous waters and hostile isles. And as he moved on pressed by a need in his soul, a hope stole through the heart of those left behind. A hope that the storms can be weathered, the rough waves tamed and the great sea conquered.

The Two Gospels of Prahlad and Hiranyakashyap

The story of Prahlad and his father Hiranyakashyap is well known. The father, born of an asuric birth wanted to attain immortality so that he could become the sole monarch of the world. But it was the monarchy of his giant ego by whose shadow he wanted to swallow the world. He wanted to eliminate all possible sources of death in his personal life. He had a beautiful child called Prahlad. He wanted to teach his child that he, Hiranyakashyap, is greater than God, the Lord of the universe.

Though the child loved his father, he did not believe his idea. He believed that Lord Hari was God and not his father. His father tried various means to force this idea on the child but when Prahlad refused to accept it, he was enraged. He tried various means to kill the child, by throwing him off the cliff, sending a snake to bite him, setting fire around him, but the child somehow was always saved by his simple faith and fearlessness. The father was getting more and more enraged at this till finally one day he decided to confront the child himself.

Threatening him to death, he asked, "tell me who is greater, myself or Hari?" "Hari" was the child's sweet and simple reply.

"Why do you say so, you stupid boy? Don't you see I am your father, the great King Hiranyakashyap, ruler over the three worlds, whom neither gods nor men, neither animals nor elements can kill, who has conquered Space and Time."

The child fearlessly replied, "But father, Hari is everywhere. He is also beyond Space and Time and can take any form as He pleases. He is in everything."

The father fumed at this reply. Pointing to an iron pillar in his royal hall, he mockingly asked his son, "Oh so he is everywhere and in everything. So is he in this pillar too for very soon I intend to make this iron pillar red hot and tie you there?"

The child looked at the hot pillar and saw a little ant crawling over it. And with all his faith, he replied, "yes, Hari, my Lord, is in the pillar too."

Now Hiranyakashyap's rage went beyond his control. He took his mace and started hitting the pillar. Each time he hit the pillar he would angrily ask, "Where is Hari, where is Hari? Show me, show me, where is Hari?"

Suddenly, the iron pillar broke up. And lo! Indeed Hari stepped out of the hot iron pillar in the form of Narsingh, the lion-man. A fight ensued and Hari as Narsingh destroyed Hiranyakashyap and enthroned Prahlad as the king over daityas.

The story, short and simple as it runs, is one of the many fascinating symbolic tales that have come out of Indian thought and Spiritual vision and experience. In the story, the king of the three worlds, Hiranyakashyap, is the giant ego that rules over the kingdom of mind, life and body so long as man lives in an asuric consciousness. The gospel of the ego is that there is no Truth, no God. All is simply matter and material energy, and everything is meant to serve the interest of the human ego.

According to Hiranyakashyap's gospel, man can conquer death by mastering the outer forces of material nature. This is the gospel that we are teaching in our schools and colleges even today. The result is a greater and greater external control over material nature and physical space and time. Also an increasing domination of the human vital ego, increasing anger, frustration, a self-destructive and world-destructive frenzy that is intolerant of other views and ideas.

However, as a saving Grace, man has in him not only the ego-self but also the soul or his spiritual-self. This spiritual-self in him comes later, when the ego-self has hardened and is ready to fall like a crust, just as the outer and harder coat of the seed must break and release the inner seed. This spiritual-self in us, that is seemingly born out of the ego-self, is Prahlad, the child-divine. He is full of trust and devotion, direct knowledge, faith and surrender. He is fearless, full of peace, sweetness and joy. He knows that this universe is not mere matter but behind it, there is the stable unchanging soul of Power and Love, Hari. He is seated in the heart of Time that uncoils infinitely; He is seated in the heart of Space upholding the cosmos and its million energies the image of Vishnu so beautifully conjured in the Puranas. This is the gospel of Prahlad, the soul within us.

For a long time, the soul lives under the shadow of the ego. But slowly it begins to assert itself. Once that starts happening, our being becomes a battlefield of conflict between the ego and the soul, between doubt and a spiritual worldview that holds and delivers matter out of itself. Sometimes one view predominates, sometimes another. The ego tries to destroy the soul and tests its faith but the soul is indestructible. The weapons cannot cleave it; nor can fire destroy it, as the Gita tells us.

Then the decisive hour arrives, the last ordeal, the test before the victory. It is then that Hari, the Friend and Lord of all beings manifests Himself in us as a leonine figure, the lion-man, Narsingh. For, it indeed needs a calm courage to overthrow the ego and offer its throne to the soul. This, indeed, is true bravery and heroism, to face our ego and destroy it so that all in us may belong to Hari, the Divine Truth, Wisdom, Power and Love behind this world. Then Hari gives back this kingdom to the soul who must then govern our life, thoughts, emotions and the very body in the name of 'Hari' and make them beautiful and perfected instruments for God's work in the world.

These are the two gospels that the world has known. So far, the human race has largely followed the way of Hiranyakashyap's gospel except for a few individuals, here and there, who have discovered Prahlad within them. No wonder the world is what it is today, full of greed and falsehood, governed by wars for domination and possession, ruled by vanity, fear, anger and death. But the time is coming near when Prahlad's gospel would appear in every home in the form of children who would challenge the old materialistic view and a world-order full of hypocrisy, division and falsehood, built by the ego for the satisfaction of our vanity. More and more children will have the courage to seek Truth, to question the human ills born of our ego, even if it wears the garb of religious or secular ideologies. Hiranyakashyap will be vanquished from the face of the earth lifting the shadow from its face. The world and Nature will be once again reclaimed and ruled by Truth, Light, Sweetness and Love.

The Flute Player

The charming flute-player had bewitched the whole village. Men and women of all ages flocked around him as his lips blew through the bamboo reed. As his gentle fingers ran over the holes wild animals became docile and flowers danced with joy under his magic spell. Even the sun and rain seemed to obey the rhythm of his music. Some enjoyed the sheer magic of his flute and cared not to analyse. Others tried to understand its method and process. The scientifically minded even tried to gather all the associated things as evidence linking them to his flute-playing capacity. They studied the quality of bamboo and the size of the flute with the spacing of holes and the force of his breath moving through it. The simple, religious minded observed his lifestyle, his eating habits, his sleep and his routine. Thereby they could emulate some of these to stimulate in themselves the capacity to play flute.

Then the flute player disappeared one day. To where none could say. But he had left behind his flute. The village after waking up to the sudden loss was divided into different systems and philosophy each claiming its right over the flute-player's fortune. Creeds sprang up, each claiming sole authority over the flute-player. Cults and rituals began in his name, where every adherent was expected to religiously follow the lifestyle of the great master. The flute was wrapped in silk and gold for the eyes of the faithful to worship. Few privileged ones (privileged in the eyes of the caretakers) got the rare opportunity to touch the flute with their fingers. In time the legacy turned into a flute religion. Each faithful member was expected to keep a flute in a worship room, wrapped in fine silk. The poor could do it in glazed cotton though. The flute was taken out of the silk cover annually in a mass festival called the bamboo-festival. The traditional ones worshipped flutes of different sizes made of bamboo alone. The modernists changed with times and flutes of fibre glass, metal and plastic with machine-art adorned their houses. The philosophers mocked the ritualists. They saw in the flute a symbol of great cosmic rhythm. They discovered and wrote books on the great seven cosmic rhythms and principles that governed life everywhere. Out of these seven rhythms sprang up the seven great laws. The hard core practicalists converted these laws into fixed and inflexible rules that all must follow. Anyone trying for any variation in the rhythm was regarded as a deviant member to be socially shunned or punished. The scientists laughed at both—the ritualists as well as the philosophers. They saw in the flute-player's magic nothing but a clever play of harmonics. They classified these harmonics into precise mathematical formulas. They calculated the rare statistical probability of the events linked to the magic of his flute. They hypothesized how the sound of the flute drove the wind in a certain way that changed the pattern of the weather and, thereby, favourably affected the crops.

Days went by and centuries and generations. The flute-player's magic turned into a hard religion, his free force into a system of philosophy, his creative art into a precise technique. Even worse, the rarity of the event turned many believers sceptics and, in collusion with the scientifically minds, they declared it all a myth and a legend believed by petrified minds.

The flute-player's soul watched all this with great pain. For all of them had caught only an outermost fringe of his clothing.

And what they all missed was his delight that he longed to share with all and the source inspiration that he wished to awaken in others so that the magic could dwell in every heart. And so, he decided to come back again. But this time he was born in another land and wore another dress. He spoke another language and had a different lifestyle. Times had changed but these things had little significance for the flute-player since he could draw the same force of inspiration and breath the same delight in every age. But people failed to recognize him. The religionists banned his entry into their citadels declaring him an infidel, a breaker of sacred traditions. The philosophers failed to understand the new music he brought to life in his creative freedom and declared him a heretic and a revolutionary. The scientists once again started analysing with their lens and their calculators. But the children followed him, entranced by his magic and the flowers once again danced with joy and the wind felt thrilled and the sun once again kissed the earth and greeted it with the freshness of a new dawn.

Ravana, the Fall from Grace

The Ramayana is an evolutionary parable that moves at several levels. At the very outset, it is very clearly a story of the conflict between the forces of Darkness and Light, with the eventual victory of Light over Darkness, Truth over Falsehood, Good over Evil. That is the memory the great epic stirs in the minds of the Indian people. But the story is not as simple as that.

Ravana, the protagonist of Darkness is not all Evil. There are traits in him that are the marks of goodness. He looks after his subjects well and has ensured for them a happy and prosperous kingdom. He also engages in religious activities and can be very generous if he is pleased. He also follows some strict rules of conduct, even if they are few and personal to him, and follows them religiously. Besides, he is a talented musician and an intellectual giant who is well versed in the scriptures. But herein lies the beauty of the epic. All these human achievements, remarkable though they may look, do not make him a godly being. Rather, he continues to bear upon him the stamp of the Asura, the fallen angel who has deviated from the path of Light. For, as the story goes, Ravana was once an angel, a watch-guard to the doors of the great Lord Vishnu, the preserver aspect of God. But he suffers a fall, a fall from grace that comes about through a curse of a sage when Ravana questions his credentials and obstructs his way to the Lord with arrogance and haughtiness that is unbecoming of God's servants. And that brings the fall, that is the stamp that Ravana carries through three lives till he is redeemed by the Grace of his Master, Lord Vishnu.

The hallmark of Ravana through all that he does is wanton arrogance and vanity that is reflected even in his seeming virtuosity. It is he who is the saviour, the protector, the winner of battles, the devotee of Shiva. He can, or so he thinks, even outdo his Lord by his strength and force till Shiva humbles him as he tries to carry the destroyer of evil along with his consort and his abode to his kingdom on his bare hands. He is a worshipper of Force and Strength and knows no other Godhead. Therefore, he distorts the great Vedic mantra Sohamasmi, That is me, to mean that the ego is That since the only self he knows is the self of the ego. It is this gigantic ego that is the mark of a Titan and not his lineage or capacities or intellectual powers or even religiosity. Of course, his intellectual capacity saves him to an extent from being an inferior form of titan, the Rakshasa, who is an image of a devouring being of some vital world, who is thoughtless and crude in his ways. Ravana, though not outright crude, is full of deceit and cunning and cannot tolerate any affront to his ego. He refuses to hear any other voice except the voice of his ego.

Since he refuses to surrender his ego, his redemption can therefore come only through a breaking of the thick shield in which his soul is trapped. His soul still longs to be God's menial and knowing the troubled and restless nature that houses it, the soul of Ravana chooses to hurl itself against God in a wrestle since this alone, it feels, can hasten the advent of its Lord and be released from this evil bondage to an accursed and fallen life of being the Adversary in God's world.

He too, therefore, serves a purpose in God's mysterious scheme of things. By his triumphant egoism, by his force threatening to destroy the sages, the gods, the guardians and keepers of the laws, Ravana hastens the advent of God into this world. By this advent, not only he but the entire clan of Asuras and Rakshasas is redeemed. Thus, evil too hastens in its own way the advent of God. And what really is evil but a deviation of the energies given to us, from their true purpose, that of serving the Lord in all humility and surrender. This is the truth of Ravana's life: A life centred around the ego is a dark and fallen life even if it is full of outer triumph and successes, even if we hide in the garb of high intellectuality and a show of religiosity, even if the person concerned is full of talent and capacities. He is still an inferior type and his soul feels stifled, entrapped and longs to be God's servant once again. For, in the final analysis, it is better to be God's slave than be a boastful and egoistic king of the three worlds, it is better to seek His service than nurture the ambition of ruling men.

When such a nature reaches its extreme it becomes the conscious harbinger of evil. Once this happens then there are only two possibilities left for it. Either to surrender to God and be converted into Light by His touch of Grace, the longer and more arduous but more fulfilling path. Or, and that is what Ravana chooses, be dissolved by the Light by hurling itself against it, a shorter but inferior path since it brings back the soul denuded and unfulfilled.

Ravana was given the choice till the last moment, even his brothers were given this choice. But it is only Vibhisana who chooses the path of surrender while the rest simply chose to dissolve back into the Light leaving the soul's mission upon earth unfulfilled, its work half-done.

The Great Flood

The earth was overrun with floods and only a few had survived. King Manu had laboured hard to save as many as he could in the gigantic boat which rocked through the waters amidst unprecedented heavy rains. It was his duty to defend his subjects and he was doing it ably enough. A dream vision had forewarned him about the imminent catastrophe. He had seen in his dream a fish grow to a huge size carrying the boat tied to a projection above its nose. The fish had appeared in successive dreams and cautioned about the great floods during which his wisdom, grit and determination will all be tested to the utmost. His task was to rescue his people and the Vedas.

It took a week-long effort to build the boat. But who was to be picked up and who to be left behind, he wondered. As the king he was duty bound to treat all as equal and could not possibly be partial in his choices. The floods had not yet started but the boat was ready. Not knowing what to do next, he spread the word around about his dream. People had to come near the river shore and then they would be taken onboard the boat starting with women and children and boatmen and those well versed in the knowledge of the scriptures and the warriors followed by the rest, space permitting. He then offered everything to the great Lord and waited for the fated morning to arrive.

The daybreak arrived but there was nothing unusual. It seemed like any other day. Though the word had been spread only a few had come trusting the vision of the king. The rest simply laughed at him. Oh! how can one trust an inner revelation that no other person had? Some thought he has gone mad. Only a few gathered who knew that the king was not only pious but also a truthful man fully devoted to the great Lord. It was quite natural then that the great Lord would appear before him to help his subjects. So they came and waited.

As the day went down and most homes had turned off the lamps, clouds began to gather suddenly and unexpectedly. The winds moved at hurricane speed and thick drops of rain started pouring like javelins from the sky.

'Let us not wait for the river to swell more. Let us set the sail.' The king and his trusted men shouted. But their voices were lost in the speeding winds and the boat was beginning to rock. Quickly the few who had gathered, tied by their faith in the king and the great Lord, went up the boat and set the sails. The younger among them started rowing the boat that rocked like a fragile toy upon the mighty river swell. It was still the thick of night, an unending night as it would seem since the clouds covered the sun above while the water spread covering the earth below. All who had chosen to stay on fixed grounds were drowned.

Meanwhile the boat kept rocking as if it would sink any moment. But always a mysterious hand seemed to save it. Seven days and seven nights they steered driven by the power of faith.

At the end of the seven days, the select few chosen by fate found the sun slowly showing up from behind the clouds. The boat had also reached ashore a place largely covered with snow with some land and scant vegetation around. It looked bereft of life, animals or men. King Manu, who always led by example and from the front, got down to see if there is any possibility of settling down there. He had very thoughtfully brought in the boat some cattle and seeds and saplings of trees that could give fruits and grain. But first he had to ascertain if the terrain was hospitable.

He went very far from the shore and ship before his eyes met a hermit or a seer sitting quietly in an ingathered state. Seeing the king, the Rishi smiled and greeted him saying that he had been waiting for his arrival.

The king was surprised with joy to learn that a greater Plan was aiding him in his journey.

How could the Rishi know, he thought for a moment, but knew also that the rishis had access to knowledge through a different kind of sense and operations of the intuitive mind that they had evolved through yoga. Was he also not shown by the great Lord the coming of the cataclysm? He who rescued his kind had already ensured that he would find their new home. Manu sought guidance and wisdom from the Rishi, sitting at his feet in a state of humility.

The Rishi started to reveal the secrets he was waiting to impart. "The earth had grown burdened," he started. "The evil hidden in the underbelly of life had raised its head and was polluting the mind space with falsehood, doubt, fear and greed. The earth goddess needed to change her worn out garb exploited by human greed. The great flood that drowned the earth was a thorough cleansing and purification. Now that the bath is over, she is ready to wear a new gown again."

When Rishi paused, Manu wondered what really is earth and why must she go through such gigantic destruction. He had heard of previous pralayas but never imagined that he will witness and, even survive, one of them.

The Rishi knew before the king could speak and continued. "Though there are countless planetary systems and countless gods and goddesses who govern the cosmos as cosmic managers, yet earth is a very special formation," he said. "It is here that the great drama of evolution is unfolding through which consciousness climbs creating new forms for the habitation of the great Lord until this creation becomes one with the Creator."

"Who then is the Creator? Is He Brahma, the bearer of the Word, or Vishnu, the powerful and Wise? Or Shiva, the mighty or the bewitching Krishna?" the king asked.

The Rishi replied, "O king, Brahma and Vishnu, Shiva and Krishna are but four aspects of the One Great Lord. They represent the Great Lord's aspects of Existence, Consciousness, Force and Delight. That is why the wise call Him as Sachchidanand. Call Him by any Name and He responds since He dwells in every creature and responds to the truth in their hearts."

The king was silent for a while contemplating on the great mysterious One, whom the wise call by many names each representing one quality or the other of His Infinity.

Then breaking the silence with a thought from afar he asked, "Here upon earth we see that everything is in pairs. So I carried pairs of animals and my fellow humans. But does the One has not His companion? How does He create?"

The Rishi explained, "Though One and Nameless, the One becomes two for the purposes of creation. They are the two principles of creation that we find everywhere, masculine and feminine, purusha and prakriti, Brahman and Maya, Ishwara and Ishwari, the Lord as the stable basis of all creation and His Shakti, the Knowledge and Power, the Conscious Force that builds, governs, penetrates, moves all creation in many worlds."

"Many worlds?" the king pondered and reflected aloud.

"Yes, O king, limited by our vision we believe the material world to be the only one. But there are countless worlds built of a different substance, worlds of the immortal Gods that are full of splendour and light, and in their contrast and opposites, worlds of the Titans, dark and dangerous."

"But why did the gracious Lord built the dark and dangerous worlds?" the king asked as the image of a terrible shadow was recalled by him during the great voyage. It was as if a gigantic shadowy being was constantly rising from the sea to drown their boat. But the great Lord rescued it safely through the stormy turbulent waters.

"Out of love He creates," the Rishi continued, "Out of love He throws challenges as the Night across the path of the immortal Soul so that it may grow wiser and strong even as the Lord."

The king contemplated and saw how every difficulty had only helped him grow stronger so that he could steer his people through this tremendous crisis. But this was only the beginning of a long new journey, he thought and the Rishi again responded to the unspoken word held back in the king's mind.

"O king indeed all destruction is the prelude to a new and higher creation. Therefore, you must rebuild a new world here and then spread out everywhere so that mankind does not make the same mistake again and bring their civilization once again to the brink of destruction." The Rishi paused and the king anxious to know asked, "But I have little resources left. How then shall we build?"

"The outer resources are but means, O king!" the Rishi spoke, "Discover the power, the infinite Shakti, the Divine Mother and build with Her Wisdom and Power, the same Power that has built this rainbow-hued creation."

"But where shall I find Her? By what means shall I seek Her?" asked the king.

"Find Her in your heart, O king, where She resides permanently. Find Her through love, it is through love that She has woven the stars as necklace around the Unseen Lord."

The Rishi closed his eyes and a Voice filled the king's heart with hope and joy and his soul heard in the deep quietude of the snow.

We are but sparks of that most perfect fire,
    Waves of that sea:
From Him we come, to Him we go, desire
    Eternally,
And so long as He wills, our separate birth
    Is and shall be.
Shrink not from life, O Aryan, but with mirth
    And joy receive
His good and evil, sin and virtue, till
    He bids thee leave.
But while thou livest, perfectly fulfil
    Thy part, conceive
Earth as thy stage, thyself the actor strong,
    The drama His.
Work, but the fruits to God alone belong,
    Who only is.
Work, love and know,— so shall thy spirit win
    Immortal bliss.
Love men, love God. Fear not to love, O King,
    Fear not to enjoy;
For Death's a passage, grief a fancied thing
    Fools to annoy.
From self escape and find in love alone
    A higher joy.

Seek Him upon the earth. For thee He set
  In the huge press
Of many worlds to build a mighty state
  For man's success,
Who seeks his goal. Perfect thy human might,
  Perfect the race.
For thou art He, O King. Only the night
  Is on thy soul
By thy own will. Remove it and recover
  The serene whole
Thou art indeed, then raise up man the lover
  To God the goal.

Sri Aurobindo: The Rishi

The Test of Fire

Sita, the daughter of earth, conceals herself before the Lila of the Lord begins in the forest. Ravana could not have come near her if she did not conceal herself and become powerless and weak. The first sign of this self-concealment is that she is lured by the unusual trick of the golden deer and refuses to listen to Rama's counsel. She is abducted by the demon king and kept a captive in his kingdom where she spends her days remembering her Lord.

A great battle then ensues and she is released following the victory of Rama. She is all set to meet him but she must walk upon fire to prove her fitness before the reunion! Our modern mind naturally does not understand and revolts. But to one on the path of yoga the symbol is very clear. Sita or Nature is one, the Shakti or Power of the Lord, but conceals and diminishes Herself to become this earthly nature. Her Power is hidden from her own sight and therefore, she is lured by appearances, the golden deer.

The soul wanders in pursuit of this illusory goal, while in the process the demoniac or asuric forces are attracted to her and seek to possess her by force. Sita refuses to yield as we all must and even while in captivity spends her days remembering her Lord. A fierce battle is then waged in our nature between the forces of a higher Light and of Darkness. The Lord wins but there is still one more test that our fallen nature must pass so that it can ascend to a supernature and be one with its Lord. It is the test of inner purification, the test of our sole allegiance to the Lord and Master of our being, the test of our sincerity and faithfulness to the Supreme. Thus redeemed our nature and re-wedded to our Lord finds its supreme consummation.

Sri Krishna and the Seven Seers

The seven seers, who guide the world from their celestial homes, had gathered at Sri Krishna's home in the eternal Vrindavan. The seven seers had come to voice their concerns over the growing menace of Ravana, the king of Lanka. He was destroying the doors of yajna and his lust and ambition were upsetting not only the balance of earth but also of celestial beings whose wealth and powers he had forcibly captured through arduous *tapasya*.

"When will the reign of the overambitious Asura end?" was the question that everybody had in their hearts. The guides of the world could not see any near solution to the problem. They cast their gaze through loops of time, only to be baffled. So, they thought of meeting Krishna, the Divine who dwells in every heart.

Krishna greeted them with his heart-charming smile. He knew their hearts and responded with an answer as enigmatic as his smile.

"But who would replace the Asura, tell me O sages bright? It has taken an aeon to replace the Rakshasa in man with the Asura. Let him then perfect the Asura in man before he falls." Sri Krishna remarked.

"What then is his source of strength? Is it his bhakti for his chosen deity Shiva?" the sages asked.

"Shiva's strength indeed he holds. But since he misuses the gift divine, he writes his own doom through his acts," Sri Krishna answered.

"What is the mantra he invokes? Pray tell us his secret," requested the seers.

And Krishna once again, "He knows that he is God, *sohamasmi*. So, he marches with confidence filled with the power of this mantra."

"Then how shall he fall?" the sages asked.

"Fall he will for he knows only half the truth. He knows not that all, all indeed is God." Krishna smiled.

And as the Lord smiled, the sages looked down upon earth and saw Ravana performing a *Rakshasic yagya* torturing his body and asking the boon for aggrandizing his ego that he mistook for the true Self.

As he offered his head in the flames Shiva appeared as Kali and bid him stay.

"'Grant me immortality," the Asura thundered.

Kali, the fierce and fearsome goddess of the Titans and the Gods, laughed and her laughter filled the world with terror and joy.

"Immortality is not for you since you mistake the body for the soul. Ask another boon," Kali retorted.

Then God in the Asura spoke seeking for the boon from the Mother of the worlds.

"Grant me then this boon that may I fall only to the animal man or a man who has fully subdued the Asura in him."

"So be it!" Kali thundered and vanished.

And as Ravana rose from his sacrifice, the sages knew the Lord's evolutionary plan. The animal man and the higher human type must replace the Asura even as he had replaced the dreaded Rakshasa.

Sri Krishna smiled and in the heart of Ayodhya, Prince Rama, the eldest son of Dasaratha, woke up in the royal palace. Sage Viswamitra had arrived to take him and his brother Lakshmana to train them for their mission.

Hope then stole in the heart of earth. The vanara of Kishkindhaa rejoiced not knowing the cause of the happiness they felt.

The Ways of Nature

The white and the black ant met one day on their way to their respective hiding grounds.

Looking disdainfully at the black ant, the white one remarked, "How underdeveloped is your ant civilization. Though we are of the same stock of ants, see how we have developed." Saying so, the white ant started bragging about its termite city that had huge high-rise mounds that looked impressive and completely shielded from the sun. They were weatherproof and the entire colony was so well organized that it was near impossible to wipe them out. The black ant had nothing to compare with, as it lived in small hideouts adapting and adjusting to the ways of nature. All that it could communicate was that outer success alone does not matter. The white ant differed saying that nature favours the aggressive and the successful. They alone survive since they are strong and capable, the fittest of the ants. The black ant was not ready to give in so easily. Taught by the ways of Nature on which they depended rather than their outer prowess alone, the black ant said:

"Look at the tiger. Strong and powerful, it has all that is needed to survive. And then look at the deer, swift footed with beautiful eyes yet an easy game for the tiger. See how Nature has worked in ways that the tiger is a threatened species whereas the deer continues to multiply."

The white ant seemed unconvinced. As a gesture of superiority, it even invited the black ant to stay in its termite city for a few days and enjoy the coolness and comfort.

The wise black ant refused but, in the passing, remarked, "Great and successful you may be but what is the use of such a success that human homes dread your arrival whereas I am welcomed by them as a sign of good fortune. Your city is built by devouring the very wood that shelters you, whereas we enrich the soil that gives us space."

So saying it quietly lugged along its way. The white ant wondered for a moment at the words of wisdom in their parting but soon walked its way with an air of vanity at the achievements of their kind. As it walked Nature, the great mother of all creatures, smiled and gently whispered to the soul of earth, "I have shared something of my intelligence and power with all my creatures but I have made a rule of the game. They who live only for themselves shall perish whereas they who live with the sense of the whole shall survive and grow."

And as she, thus, whispered these words of wisdom, the King of Lanka heard it not and continued to build his termite city with stolen wealth and the blood of earth's creatures. But at the other end of Bharatvarsha, the gentlest, yet mightiest of all, Rama of the Ikshvaku clan smiled as if nodding to Mother Nature in assent, reassuring her that the Lord of Nature has come to uphold the law and the rule of the game. The days of the devouring Rakshasa and the Asura were numbered. But the animal kind, from the monkey to the bear would have the glory of aiding the ascent of man.

The Journey: A Fable of the Two Paths

The little fish, Dino, was happy in its little pond. It was a small and secure world where every fish practically knew every other fish. There were just a few varieties of them and, except for some minor variations, they all looked alike. Since they had very similar lives and problems, they perhaps even thought alike. The only risk for them was the angler at the banks and the fishermen with their nets. To escape from the former, they had learnt to stay near the middle and not stray too far towards the banks. The silent rule they all understood and faithfully followed was that safety lies in staying within the limits of the pond and curiosity and exploration were the cause of all catastrophes. But for the latter danger, they had little recourse. They could not get the better of man's deception and the greed for food that led them to the net. Though here again they tried to reduce their chances of being caught by staying in groups. Their safety lay in numbers or that's what they thought. But when one of them was caught, the others simply learned to resign to their fate.

Though Dino grew up amidst this lot, yet she was different from the very start. To begin with she was somewhat smaller than the rest. Her smaller size and a little unusual patch of outgrown flesh upon her fins made her somewhat different and unique and, therefore, also somewhat isolated and lonely. For though nature revels in creating variations, her individual types do not tolerate variations beyond a point. They either condemn him or admire and worship but secretly feel that the variant is an anomaly that was to be dreaded and shunned in practice. Nevertheless, she had reconciled to her fate even though she secretly nurtured dreams of another fish world with many varieties and forms of fishes, some amazingly huge and powerful, some amazingly beautiful and wonderful. Yet she would not speak of her dreams to anyone lest she became an object of ridicule and was openly declared unfit to live in the fish world. Such things were after all dreams and imagination, which some mad fishes would have but not the saner and safer ones. For, in that small little fish world, sanity was equated with safety, wisdom with the ability to remain fixed to the type and truth and reality with the limits of the present.

But Dino could not stop dreaming and at the slightest pretext she would withdraw from her small and neat little fish world to dwell upon the object of her imagination. Till one day she was so lost in her reverie that the borders of the reality of her small fish world was over-passed and she stepped into another place and world, a world where there was water everywhere without any shore. "Oh! How huge is this pond," she thought at first. But there was nothing of the pond familiarity in that vast waterbody except that both had water. As she sat gazing and wondering, she saw a form unknown to her approach. It was a strange being, half fish with tail fins but the upper half looked like the reflection of some fishermen. But she felt no fear for the approaching being, who rather seemed all love and wisdom. The strange form noticed the perplexity and wonder in Dino's eyes and spoke answering her curiosity. "I am your future and your destiny. It is I who sent you the dreams and the imaginations." Looking at the amazement in Dino's eyes, she further spoke:

"I am a mermaid; the god of the sea world and I govern the life of all fishes. But now I have come to tell you something else. Very soon your neat and safe world is going to be destroyed in a flood that I have decided to send for you."

"For me, the flood?" the little fish was even more perplexed. She had only heard about all-destroying floods that had upset everything in the remote pasts of her ancestors. "But did you not say you were a god!"

The mermaid smiled: "Yes, and I will send you the flood since I love you very much."

"But why? Won't it destroy many a fish and what good will flood do to me anyway?"

There was this time a tinge of apprehension in Dino's eyes.

"What good does your remaining stuck in a pond does anyway? So, I have decided to take you to your place of high destiny and, hence, the flood. But fear not when the waters swell and all seems lost, I shall carry you where you are destined to be and make of you what you have always dreamt and secretly wished to be, since it was I who thus dreamt and wished in you," replied the mermaid.

The tone of the mermaid seemed at once commanding and reassuring. But the little fish questioned one last time. "But is a flood necessary? Can't I find my destiny without this great and all-upsetting and frightful deluge?"

"No, without the flood you can only dream about it, for you do not have the strength to follow your dream and reach where you must. Your little fins cannot carry you so far. Hence, I am sending the flood. Remember, do not fear, rather trust, surrender and wait. The flood may look fierce but it is actually my force that comes to break your limits and thus set you free."

So saying, the sea-god vanished and in her trail left a lingering joy mixed with anticipation in the little fish. Her words kept echoing in her dream, "Remember, do not fear, rather trust, surrender and wait."

* * *

And she waited and a few more days passed. These days were full of strange forebodings. The fish world was witnessing unexpected things. With each passing day the little fish would grow restless about the coming event. She even wondered if what she saw was true and not another of her imaginations. And so it went on till the day of destiny arrived. It seemed a clear day like any other day and the little fish world was busy with its little things and familiar world of everyday life. And then suddenly all was changed. The suddenness of the event left no room for anything at all. The fish world collapsed, got swallowed in that sudden and mighty upsurge of water. All was over within a few moments that seemed like eternity. And when the little fish stunned by the shock and carried by the large wave came back to its senses, she found herself in sweet and strange waters of a stream that must have existed nearby but was till then unknown to her little fish world. As she began orienting herself, she observed what magnificent variety of creatures lived there, some were like the fish but colourful and beautiful, others were strange inhabitants of the freshwater stream that was clear and limpid.

"How strange is this world," she thought. But the next moment wondered how she and the other fishes had lived so long without even knowing that such a beautiful world existed nearby. But then as if in a flash something else caught her imagination. "If there existed such a world nearby yet unknown to me then where are the limits? Is this the end, the place of my destiny or do I explore and go further?" She swam with this thought day in and day night till one day she dreamt again. She did not see the mermaid this time but only heard her all familiar voice tell her, "Trust your dream. Did I not say that I sent them to you? Go further if you feel that further exists."

Further to where, she thought and as if something within her own being replied to her: "Follow the current and the stream will lead you to its source and its secret."

And so her journey continued till the stream began to swell and she could feel something approaching where the world of the stream ended and another world began. At first little Dino grown a little more drinking the sweet waters of the lovely stream, tumbled into the river catapulted by a massive force that shook her again. Fear overtook her, this time more than the first time for she did not have the surety of the vision. It was not any angelic being telling her to move but something within her that had impelled her to explore further. Was she right to listen to this impulse? Were not her family and tribe members right that one should not tread unknown territories; that only in limits are we safe? All these questions flashed before her even as she fell over a waterfall into the river. The very sense of something far more powerful and wider was as if frightening. But then she remembered again, "Do not fear, rather trust, surrender and wait." But it was not easy out there. The current was too strong, the water quite cold, the riverbed too deep for comfort and the inhabitants not only strange but a few of them frighteningly huge for her small stature. For a while she thought if it was worth journeying further, if the stream world to which she has grown accustomed, and which was beautiful, was not the perfect world of her dreams, her highest destiny. Yet, something within her compelled to go further, something within her would not go back, something within wished to go to the very end of this interesting journey into the unknown and the unexplored, into this adventure of a new, a dangerous yet charming, world whose last secret she wished to know. But what was the path to follow from here, the path that would lead her to the last secret, to some greater world of her dreams.

Thus, musing she spent a few days whence she chanced upon a strange creature that could move in and out of water at will. This was truly strange, an impossible thing for the fish. *How could this creature live without the life-giving water*, she thought. The creature appeared harmless and often retreated in a shell-like structure that it carried over its head as if shy of the other inhabitants of the river.

* * *

One day Dino dared to approach it. "Who are you, oh great sir, I truly admire your capacities that I have not. Could you teach me how to live without water?" She blurted all her questions at once.

"They call me the tortoise and I am simply endowed with this capacity to breath in water and outside it. There is nothing special about it, to me at least, since that's how I am made. And since I did nothing to make myself the way I am, I cannot teach you the secret of being this way as I frankly do not know it myself."

Dino was a little disappointed at the simple and straight confession of the tortoise who seemed nothing short of a miracle to the fish. But she was encouraged by his truthfulness to ask further. She knew he would not deceive her. So she ventured to ask if he knew where the source of this river was and wither it goes. "Pray tell me great sir, if you know the course of this river and where to it flows. I see no end to its waters and though for days I have tried to find its end, I have miserably failed. I can span its width and know the shores but then is the river endless in its onward flow?"

The tortoise became pensive and after a while replied: "Perhaps, I know something of that since I have seen many a season and in my long life I have met many creatures, some of whom have spoken to me of the river's flow." Then, falling silent for a while, as if to recollect all that he knew, the sage-like tortoise spoke again. "Well, the shore is not the river's origin nor its end though many mistake it to be so. The river flows from the unseen snowy peaks of the great and mighty mountains and it ends by emptying itself into the great and mighty sea."

The tortoise paused for a while. *The sea*, something flashed like recognition before Dino. Did she not hear the mermaid tell her that she was a sea god? And she had wondered what this sea was. Now the whole thing came back again and with it the thrill of her vision and the dreams of another world. "Pray tell me about the sea, oh great one," she hastened to ask.

"Ask me not of the sea since I have only heard of it and, hence, I should not speak of it to you. I only know that there is a sea, but it is an indirect knowledge. All that I can tell you is that there are two paths you can take from here."

"The two paths," asked Dino, "and what are they?"

"Well, the two paths are the path of annihilation and the path of fulfillment." The former takes you back to the origin of the river, to high mountain, but you cannot reach the snow summits there. You would, as you travel along this path become more and more alone as few creatures can survive in that cold. Then one day you would simply fall away from your fish nature."

"And what does that mean?" asked Dino.

"Oh, that's one way to die and finish yourself, one way to exit the journey. But do not ask me where you go from there once you drop your fish nature. Perhaps you simply merge with the spirit of the mountains, perhaps you come back again. Who knows, but one thing is sure, and it is this, that you will cease to exist as a fish thereafter, at least that is what it seems. But I do not know further."

"And where does the other path lead me to, the path of fulfillment?"

"That leads to the door of your destiny. As you go through this path you would find more and more fishes accompanying you, some of them much bigger and more powerful than you or any you have known. And then, if you persist you would reach the sea. But I do not know what you would find there for I know nothing about the sea. Only one thing I know and it is this that while both paths are difficult, the path to fulfillment is much longer though, perhaps, more satisfying," answered the tortoise.

"So would you not want to take that path, we could travel together," Dino said, a little excitedly.

"No, my dear friend, each of us has our road to travel. The Spirit of Nature has given me a long life but it has not given me the seeking. I am satisfied with wherever I am. Some call it a great quality but personally, I wish I had the zeal and ardour, the dare and courage, the trust and faith that you have in your seeking that has led you so far. As for me, I am born here and I will die here. Even if I were to follow you, my slow nature would not allow me to go very far. But you my friend are distinctly marked to go further. Pass over us and reach where thou must." Thus saying, the tortoise fell silent and the little fish quietly reflected upon the two paths.

* * *

'To be or not to be' seemed the choice before her and this time there was no mermaid to tell her as to where the land of her destiny was. Which way should she go? The path of annulment was shorter and perhaps less arduous, but how can that be her destiny or for that matter the destiny of any fish. What was the difference between this and the fate of the fishes carried in the net of the cunning fisherman? If this was it, then why was all this labour of the fish swimming for life and in fact this fish world at all? No, the Spirit of Nature cannot be so meaningless and absurd. But then she could equally argue against her own logic by saying that *may be this is the end of the world, and the river is the highest destiny of any fish. After all, the great tortoise had not seen the sea either. Maybe he is wrong about it. Maybe there is no sea. But what about the visitation of the mermaid? No, the sea must be there but … is it worth all the trouble?* All these thoughts and counter thoughts kept her swimming furiously all the while. But then, tired of all this effort she fell silent and entered her world of dream again. She came out without remembering what she saw in her dream but one sentence or a fragment of it slipped into her waking world, "You are never given an urge without the capacity to fulfill it."

And indeed, she felt an urge to move forward through the path of fulfillment. She knew not where the urge came from but it was there all the same. In fact, it was always there and would only revive itself from time to time.

As if to give her the last push to go further, she remembered again the words that followed her like a mantra, "Do not fear…. Trust, Surrender, … Wait."

And her wait for the journey began.

* * *

At first, she knew not which way to go. The river was too big and it was difficult to say the direction in it. She asked a few but none could tell her which way was the path of self-fulfillment. She turned to the left and then turned to the right, she swam above and then swam below, but alas could not surmise which way to go. No sign came, no visions to guide, no being to help her find the pathway right. Tired and dazed of her seemingly long and meaningless search she looked flustered and spent. Oh! if only the sea-god could help her find the way but even if she would she wondered if there was strength in her to follow the long and difficult path. Confused and wondering, yet she kept up her need to explore the farthest end and her trust in destiny. And destiny did arrive, or at least the day of her destiny, but in the most unexpected way. It looked as if doom, not destiny, had come that day which had seemed like any other day. Perhaps out of tiredness, she was swimming oblivious of the net that was spread over the river by some adventurous men who were moving downstream in their steamer.

This was surely the end of the world and of all my explorations, she thought as the net tightened around her and other fishes. She felt the sharp sting of death as her whole being ached for a single breath. And yet even in that moment of doom and despair she felt a touch of sorrow that she was dying before fulfilling her need to reach the land of her dreams, the great sea. Or was it all an imagination, a rash and thoughtless adventure. And she swooned the next moment as life hung in her fainting fins by a slender thread. Meanwhile the fisherman had rolled the net and as he was going to put the fishes in his basket, he noticed this strange fish with spotted fins. What appeared as a deformity to her friends and kin appeared to this man as a rarity and wonder. In split second a thought crossed his mind that it would be more profitable to sell this little fish in an aquarium as a curio rather than in the fish market. And before even he could decide he had the fish thrown into a tub kept nearby where he had collected some such strange and rare specimen of the water world. Oh! The gasp of breath was as if the very breath of Grace in her life. Perhaps the sea-god had indeed helped her. But then she was now a prisoner unsure of her predicament. And she could do nothing. To even try jumping out of the fishbowl was certain death. Shy and afraid she waited in a corner wondering where fate would lead her next. The fishbowl was a strange world in itself. There were some peculiar creatures the kind of whom she had never seen before. There were a few turtles, some corals, some colourful fishes, and many others. Each looked confused and frightened, unsure of their fate. Yet each had a story to tell that disclosed an entirely different world to the little fish. But also, for the first time, she had a clear look at the sky and saw the stars at night. There was nothing to do but trust and wait. For the first time she learnt the meaning of surrender in its deepest sense. Indeed, unknown to her, the secret hand of destiny was leading her. In fact, she was literally being carried by the hand of destiny since the steamer was fast traveling towards the sea where the men were to disembark. What the little fish took to be a prison was indeed a net of safety meant to spare Dino the effort to do it all by herself. What she may not have been able to do, to swim through the length of the river was being done for her, even though she knew it not, till…

Till destiny led her to the end destination. But not without another jolt, though a minor one. For as the steamer hurled itself along the river, and as it approached close to the sea, a small flash storm sent everything topsy-turvy. The bowl fell down and broke in a jiffy and the raging winds swept little Dino and the other creatures into the river in a split second. Even before Dino could realize what had happened, she found herself being forcefully carried by the strong river current towards the place she was destined, the sea. Soon the river had emptied her contents, including Dino, into the sea and the little fish found herself in a very, very different world than any she had imagined so far. A world before which all her experience, and she had a considerable amount of it by now, seemed to pale—the world of the sea.

* * *

At first the sea appeared to be like any other water world, but Dino realized soon that it was very different. To begin with, the water tasted different. The next thing she felt was the enormous force that the sea contained. And very soon also that to swim here was very different than swimming in the river, the stream and the pond. Something was very different about this place which seemed like an endless mystery. For she could not see a being there, neither fish nor frog nor a tortoise, and all the creatures that she knew of. *Was this the sea?* she thought and thought till the loneliness grew frightening. The more she explored the more she felt it a fathomless mystery. Very soon she lost all orientation. But one thing she had learnt by now and it was this that when you do not know or understand what is going on around you, then trust and wait. So, she waited a seemingly endless wait till she saw a huge fish approach her. Little Dino had never seen anything of the kind before. She simply stood transfixed in a spot. But as the big fish approached, she felt something very nice about it. Her arrival did not generate any fear, but only hope, courage and trust such that the presence of strong and benevolent beings generates for those who are less endowed.

"I am Mauna, the Dolphin, a teacher of the ways of the sea. The sea-god sends me to you to welcome and carry you safely to her."

Little Dino was deeply touched. So, the sea-god knew of everything, even the movement of a small little insignificant fish, like Dino, entering into the sea, she thought.

But Mauna seemed to have read her thoughts, "Not only does the sea-god know of all who enter the great sea, she is also aware of all that have not yet arrived at the sea. She is indeed the guardian of all the creatures that dwell in the waters."

"So, you are going to teach me of the sea and its ways."

"No, I am going to teach you nothing."

"Pray, say again," asked Dino wondering if she heard it right, "did you not say that you are a teacher?"

"Yes, I did," Mauna smiled, "but it is not me who will teach you, rather it is you who will teach yourself."

"So, then what would you be doing?"

"Well, simply facilitating the process of your self-education." Noticing Dino's puzzled expression Mauna added, "See, you are a creature of the waters, hence all that you need to know about anything that has to do with the waters, including the great sea is known to you. But it is forgotten due to your birth in the little pond. You have recovered only that much knowledge of the waters as was necessary for you to live in the pond. But as you travelled through the stream and the river you have discovered the knowledge of these as well. Your journey was essentially a rediscovery of what you already know." And then after a pause he added, "Knowing is remembering. It is uncovering what you already know but have forgotten."

"But then why does one need a teacher," Dino was growing more and more inquisitive.

"Didn't I say, to facilitate the process. It is like a reminder, or to put it more accurately, the teacher is a reminder of what you are, secretly, and can be."

"You mean you are a reminder to me of what I can be?" Dino asked doubtingly, for Mauna looked far too impressive in size and capacities for her to even remotely hope to become like him.

"Yes, you are myself, but in disguise. That is what I am going to each you or rather reveal to you. Only you have been conditioned so long by the pond that you do not even admit another possibility or another way of being for you. Yet, my child, I, the guardian angel of the sea, is your destiny."

"Okay perhaps you are right, though I do not understand anything of what you say now. But I trust you and entrust myself to you. Now when and where do we begin."

"Have we not already begun." Mauna smiled.

"So, what is the first lesson that you would teach me."

"Not me teaching you, but you learning yourself," quipped Mauna and added, "The first lesson is indeed the most difficult to learn."

"And what is that?"

"It is to unlearn"

"Hmmm," the little fish mused as if half understanding it.

"The ways of the sea are very different from the ways of the static pool and the running streams and the flowing rivers. The pool has nowhere to go for it knows not anything beyond itself. And the river and the stream run helplessly to the sea. But where would the sea go? It has nothing beyond itself for it contains all things including the earth and all that grows in it."

Dino did not quite grasp the meaning.

Mauna continued, "you see the sea is everywhere and moves in all directions. You cannot know which way it moves and that can be frightening."

"Even you can't gauge its direction and movement?" asked Dino.

"No, none can know the sea, not even me, even though I am born in the sea and live day and night by the sea and even teach the ways of the sea. I can tell you some of the ways of the sea but not about the sea itself. If you ask me about the sea, I can only say that the sea is to your right and the sea is to your left and the sea is above you and the sea is within you and the sea is around and about and outside you even as the sea is within you; and you breath the sea and eat and live the sea and yet ask me not what the sea is for I know not of it."

"Will the sea god know of it?" asked Dino.

"No not even the sea god but the sea god will tell you something more about it."

"And what is that?"

"Well, I can tell you something about the ways of the sea, about its mighty force and how to be in it and live by it, but the sea god will tell you about the being of the sea. But there is one last mystery of the sea and none can talk about it. That mystery can only be lived and experienced, not talked or taught."

"And what is that mystery, I mean what is it called, is there a name to it?"

"The wise call it delight. It has no names and many names—a delight of being born in the sea, and a delight of being upheld by the sea and even a delight of being drowned by the sea."

The mystery of the sea was getting deeper and deeper. Mauna suddenly became silent and Dino was lost in a contemplative reverie. Perhaps it was the first touch of the delight that Mauna spoke of. Slowly they drifted, led by the ocean current, to Mauna's resting place covered with beautiful sea plants and coral reefs. It was time to rest.

* * *

That night Dino had a strange visitation in a dream. The Mermaid appeared again but this time it was an appalling sight. The sea god appeared to be as vast as the skies, as if she had wrapped the heaven and earth in her body. Her hairs flowed and mingled with the stars, her body occupied the mid-worlds while her lower half that resembled a fish went deep into the ocean floor and even perhaps below. The sight was wonderful and frightful at the same time. The visitation appeared for a while and then vanished. But it left a deep impact, a quivering trace, upon the body and soul of Dino. In fact, she was woken up by Mauna who simply nudged and shook her out of her reverie with these words: "Hurry! Come on get up and get ready. The sea is rising in the shape of a giant wave."

"How do you know?" asked Dino who could sense nothing unusual in the waters which seemed just as the previous day.

"No time to answer that. Just trust that I know it or to put it in another way I have special faculties that can show me things and one of them is to see an approaching storm." Mauna answered and began to swim leaving no room for further questions. He swam slowly so Dino could follow. But Dino insisted: "So where do we go when the sea rises into a stormy wave? We can't go outside the sea, can we?"

"No that would be foolish. When the storm rises, we must go deeper. The storm is on the surface, but in the depths, there is always peace and safety." And then added as if mysteriously, "the sea that destroys with one mighty sweep what it has created over centuries is also the sea that shelters and protects and saves from its fiercer mood."

Even before Dino could realize the full significance of Mauna's words, they were swept down tumbling into the ocean deep only to find themselves as suddenly in a zone of peace and safety. It seemed as if the storm never existed. It was as if the sea though one was many at the same time. It had within it zones after zones, layers after layers, guarding secrets after secrets in its deep fathomless bosom. It was a wonderful lesson that the terrible storm taught Dino, her very first lesson of the sea, or so it seemed.

* * *

The days that followed went off rather smoothly. Mauna had a wonderful way of teaching. He simply swam and inspired Dino to swim with him. Usually, he would not interfere with Dino's ways and even did not correct her mistakes. He would intervene only if Dino was in a danger. And since Mauna had this ability to sense danger from far ahead most of the time Dino did not even know that she has been saved and some danger averted! Dino learnt many interesting things about the sea. Her very first lesson was in surrender and humility. She learnt that the best way to swim in the sea was not to swim! And when you had reached the extreme level of your effort and feel you can swim no longer it is then that you feel most supported by the force of the sea. Of course, the sea supported you even without effort yet it was not the same. The effort was as if required to develop the muscles and nerves to bear the mighty force of the sea without breaking down or being disoriented. The effort helped her to simply remain in the sea, the rest was done by the sea itself. Effort was necessary to prepare her for giving full force to her surrender and to receive the full delight that follows it. Once Dino learnt this trick, she began to understand what Mauna meant when he spoke of the delight of the sea. She learned that the sea water, though salty and different in taste was as it was to help the creatures of the sea swim with minimum effort. Dino also learnt that the sea had countless creatures some huge yet gentle, others small yet dangerous, as if size was an illusion. She also learnt that the sea held all its million creatures together in its embrace without judging them and providing for each one. Most of all Dino learnt that the greatest treasures of the sea lay in its deepest parts where pearls and other invaluable gems lay hidden as if in some dark cave. Through daily contact with Mauna, her teacher, Dino spontaneously began developing some of those marvelous faculties that Mauna had and spoke of. She began to know Mauna's thoughts even before he spoke. She could communicate with the many creatures of the sea silently without a word and they seemed to listen and even obey her. Even creatures that were much too big and far too ferocious gave way to her as if to someone special and exceptional. It is then that Dino really began to understand much of what Mauna had hinted at earlier, for instance, this that size does not matter. One truly knows something only when one has experienced it oneself and not merely learnt of it from someone else. Doing is knowing. Dino learnt this by doing faithfully what Mauna inspired her by his own example. Then the day of the final lesson arrived.

That day was like any other day. Dino came out of her reverie and went for a deep-sea swim. This was one of the things that she had learnt from Mauna—to take a deep dive every morning. It refreshed her endlessly. There was so much silence and peace and force in the depths of the sea. On her return she looked for Mauna but could not find him. May be Mauna has gone elsewhere. But this was unusual. During so many days of her being with him he never kept Dino out of his reach. But today somehow Dino felt otherwise. Where was he, where had he disappeared? The anxiety grew with every passing minute. No nothing could happen to Mauna. He was a perfect master. He knew everything that had to be known and could be known about the sea. But then the sea was the unknowable. So did the sea swallow Mauna? Dino suddenly felt very unsafe, much more than she had felt either in the pond or the river even with the fishermen's net around. If Mauna could thus disappear without a word or a trace then nothing was certain and everything was fragile and vulnerable not to speak of her. She waited more but to no avail. She furiously swam in this direction and that but still to no avail. And when she had done all that she could, she simply went back to their place of rest silently in wait for the next turn of fate. She remembered her mantra that had always helped her in every crisis, "Do not fear, rather trust and wait."

* * *

Three days passed without a sign of Mauna though Dino began to sense some new change in her. She felt that her body was not the same anymore. But what was it she could not know till she saw her reflection in a floating coral whose smooth and crystal clear surface reflected everything. And this was Dino's real surprise for she had grown so much like a miniature Mauna, a little dolphin that, but for its size, had everything similar to the dolphin and even its capacities. She could not believe her eyes at first. But soon the truth began to dawn upon her. So, this was the reason why Mauna had left her. His work was over and well done and he left silently without even waiting for a word of gratitude from her, a gratitude which she always felt for him. *But then did he not say that there was one last lesson to be learnt! What was it?* wondered Dino? What was it that Mauna wanted her to decipher from his sudden departure in this way? Surely, he would not leave her without revealing all that he had to and could for Mauna was a perfect teacher and would not leave anything unfinished. So, what was Mauna trying to say for this was indeed his characteristic way of teaching, not so much through words as by example, influence and a silent inspiration. And then as she reflected on everything and, the strangest of things, a thought flashed across her being. A thought that her being and Mauna had become one. There was no more any difference between them. What was outside is now within always and permanently as her intimate self and that she had perhaps only to look within and enter into her own depths even as she entered the depths of the sea and she would find Mauna and all the answers that she got from him by turning without. Mauna and she had become essentially one.

A deep intense longing suddenly seized Dino, a longing to rediscover Mauna within her being. So far, she had related to him only as a teacher and revered him with respect and awe. But the distance created by awe and respect had suddenly vanished as the walls that separated them as two different beings crumbled. She felt an urge, something like a deep ache, to be near him who had become so very intimate to her being. In fact, if at this point someone asked what is it that she wanted most then she would say without a hesitation or doubt that it was Mauna. Without realizing he had silently grown into her nerves and cells, into the very stuff of her being, her essence and deepest truth, so much so that if she had to leave behind everything including her fish life in which she had discovered so much, she would happily do so just to have one glimpse of Mauna. The longing grew to a point of life and death. As if her entire being had grown to one single point of concentration—an aspiration that rose like a column of fire seeking for its goal in a moment of utter self-forgetfulness. For that one moment she could give up everything. Nothing else mattered except that. Without even realizing it Dino had fallen into a trance and as if in a moment of apocalypse, which seemed like eternity, she beheld before her eyes the great sea god appear again. But this time it was not as in a dream, it was right there concrete before her eyes, not an apparition but someone so very living and real, who though apart seemed to be her very breath and life. It was as if her own existence had become unreal before that wonderful reality. Or perhaps that form was the life of her life and, in fact, the life of all life. Silence fell upon her entire being. Amazement and wonder mixed with adoration and awe filled her as the lovely form spoke: "O child of the great sea! here comes the end of thy journey."

The sweet and melodious voice melted into silence again and Dino's heart replied: "O great one, my heart is seized with an intense longing for my teacher Mauna. Somewhere I know that he is me and I am him but my heart aches for him even as my being longs for the last lesson that he has left unfinished."

"But he has left nothing unfinished. This is the last lesson for which he had to leave you and disappear into your own being."

"I don't get it." Dino knew and knew not.

And the great god spoke again: "The last lesson is the lesson of love, that sweet and fierce longing that you feel for him who has hid himself in you so as to become the very essence of your being. Love that touches its peak in self-forgetfulness. Love that made Mauna loose himself in you so that you may become like him. Without this great sacrifice you could not be like him but only a shadow or a reflection."

"Does that mean that I would never find him again?"

"But have you not found him? Who do you think Mauna is, yet another fish, simply a more developed fish, a perfect fish. All that is only Mauna's shadow." And then added in a more familiar voice, "don't you see Mauna in me. It is I who came to you as Mauna. Now ask me a wish and it shall be granted." The voice was too familiar to be missed. Dino looked closely and saw in the great god's eyes a clear reflection of Mauna and all her remaining doubts had vanished. A great joy seized her being a joy as she had never known before. In an ecstasy of hope a cry broke from her as of one who having travelled very far finds the goal of her journey right in front. "O great being, I have no more wishes left having seen you and having been loved by you what more could I want but to simply merge in you and become one with your being, a part and parcel of you."

"So be it. Ask another boon, my loved child. Ask and it shall be granted."

"O great Mother, I know what it means to be a fish. I have seen the struggles and the pains of the fish life right from my birth in the little pool. Pray give me the strength to do something for my kind."

"So be it, my most dear child. Ask another boon, my favourite one. Your selfless boon makes me happy. For your own perfection would have been incomplete without the perfection of the entire fish world. Ask yet again and it shall be granted."

And a third time Dino asked the great god: "I long to be always part of your work. To serve you always and everywhere is all I ask."

"Think again my child for it may mean renouncing the bliss that you experience now. It means perhaps going back to the pond and be as a fish amidst other fishes."

But Dino replied from her very core: "Why should I fear that O my beloved one for I know now that you too would be by my side always and everywhere. Have I not already known this? Was it not you in the storm and the net, in the river and the sea? Nay in my very longings and my hopes, even in my fears and my ordeals were you not there? And now that I have known this may I never forget this at any time."

"Truly you are the very best fish of my fish kingdom and I am proud of you, my child. So be it and all else that you may ask shall be granted for you have asked the very highest that one may ask as a fish. From now on, I appoint you as one of the great teachers to do my work in the fish kingdom. And this

I promise that never shall I leave you and wherever you maybe you shall find me always by your side."

The great vision faded from her sight leaving in its wake a lingering joy that was the very essence of love. Dino started her journey back to the pool led by the sea god whom she now felt and knew everywhere. And unknown to them and their little care laden life a hope stole through the entire fish world, a hope of another way of being, a hope of a new life. The struggle of life changed its face and became for the fish world the struggle for evolution into the most perfect fish that ever could be.

Part Two
In the Master's Light

Love

"What is love?" asked a disciple of the Master. The Master replied, "Tell me, what is not love?"

And then to make it clearer he took them to the nearby fields where a farmer was tilling the soil while another was sowing seeds. Yet another was watering the plants while someone else was plucking them.

"Here look," said the Master, "the farmer who is tilling the soil is doing a labour of love even though the soil may not like this touch of hardness that it must bear, the upsetting of its layers of sand that has settled over the centuries." He continued, "And the farmer who is putting the seeds in the womb of darkness and pouring over it the waste of earth is also doing a labour of love, for the seed is still hard and must soften through all this darkness and waste till it is ready to receive the Light."

"And when it sprouts, the farmer puts a fence around it and prunes and limits its freedom lest it is eaten away by the animals that sprawl around. The delicate and tender plant may find it hard to bear the touch of his scissors but this too is love."

"And when the plant has grown and the fruits and flowers are ready, he carefully selects them and sends them away so that the flowers and fruits of his sacrifice reach out everywhere and bring new blossoms and more fruits and flowers. This too is love."

"But what about the plants and the earth?" asked another.

The Master stood silent awhile as if lost in the wonder of love that he found everywhere. When he came out of his reverie, he spoke again, "The earth holds these and many other countless possibilities silently in its bosom. It waits for the right farmer and the right season; it bears the hard touch of the farmer's plough so that one day the flowers and the fruits that it hides in the mud may emerge out of its dark womb and be offered to the sun. What else is this but love?"

"And the seed lets go of its hard crust, the plant of its shelter under the earth, its sap rising upward as an invocation to the sun and its fruits and flowers give themselves freely to the birds and the bees so that through their droppings more fragrance and more sweetness can arise out of the earth. What else is this but love?"

And the disciples stood speechless in wonder and a fresh waft of air moved amidst them, the wind that gives life force to the plant, dries up the farmer's sweat, brings about the seasons by following the paths of the sun and carries the pollen far and wide for fresh blossoms. The Master spoke not, but the disciples heard in the winds a hymn of love whisper softly a song of hope in their hearts and a renewed joy in their souls.

Truth

"Master, what is truth?" asked a disciple who had been struggling to understand this for years.

As was his method of instruction, the Master pointed towards a glass of water that was lying on the table and asked the disciple, "What is that?"

"Water of course!" replied the disciple, somewhat surprised at the suddenness and the simplicity of the question, but wondering what depth lay behind this simplicity that the Master would disclose.

"And what is water? Can someone tell me that?" the Master seemingly inquired.

One went on to describe its properties, its colour, taste, smell and so on.

And the Master probed, "But that is only what your senses perceive or report to you. That tells us about how human beings experience contact with water. So it is a relative truth and not the reality of water."

Another, who seemed like a scientist, ventured confidently, "Well, scientists have analysed the structure of water molecules and it is made up of a certain combination of hydrogen and oxygen atoms."

The Master smiled and asked him, "That is only its structure as you perceive it through your mathematical models. It tells us what constitutes the material aspect of water. But this does not tell us why this combination has certain properties and not others. It still does not explain the truth of water."

The scientist nodded in approval and added, "But this is as far as science has gone and perhaps can go."

"But not art and aesthetics, not the poet and the mystic," the Master observed turning to the rest of his disciples.

One, an artist and a poet perhaps, said, "Well, water is the giver of life because it is itself a symbol of life, ever-flowing, ever-moving, ever-changing its course, though ever the same in its depths."

The Master seemed happy with this answer but turned to a mystic who was quite indrawn as if in silent contemplation. Gathering himself, the mystic spoke, "It is a symbol of our mind that reflects the Self. If it is still, it reflects the inner truth; if it is moving and restless, it distorts it."

And another, who had developed the occult vision responded, "Water is consciousness limiting itself in certain form and functions. It is the gross representation of a subtle reality. The force of consciousness that makes things flow is the inner truth of water."

The Master smiled and even as the disciples were wondering at the many ways of looking at, perceiving and understanding water, he spoke with the authority of someone who knows something because he has made it, "All these are so many facets of the reality of water, depth upon depth, each complementing the other. Yet, even if we were, to sum up, all these things we would still miss out on the essential as well as the total truth of water. And that cannot be described in words but known only through an experience of identifying with it."

The Master fell silent and the disciples fell into a contemplative mood reflecting upon the meaning of those strange but powerful words. And as their meditation grew deeper and profound, one disciple began to enter deeper and deeper into the truth of what is known and recognised as water.

He entered past the truth of the senses. He entered deeper and went past the truth of the atomic void and its mysterious magic that lends shape and form to apparent nothingness. Further, he pressed on and saw the world of symbol figures and the flow of energy and all nature through the shape and form of water.

He went on until he met the very being of water appeared before him as the godhead who stands behind the flux and flow of the vast current of life. For a while, he felt that this was the last bedrock, the inner foundation of water. But prompted by an inner nudge he concentrated till his whole being became one with the great godhead of his vision. And he felt himself flow everywhere and become the movement of the cosmic whorl.

In the being of water, he saw all other beings grow one in unity. He saw the light of the stars and the dust of the planets; he saw the splendour of the sun and the heat and fire that built the worlds. He saw the winds raising the dead to life and again contracting them till they collapse and die. And he saw behind these godheads and their wonderful artistry, the work of a great cosmic Intelligence weaving the dance of creation. He slipped past the world of forms as if carried by some giant wave of bliss. And past that vast stupendous dance of creation, at its centre and core, he beheld the deathless One from whom all emerges and issues forth as if from an unseen womb, by whom all sustains, as if by a fixed unalterable law, to whom all returns, undone as if by a magician's skill. Rapt in his vision and full of unspeakable joy, he got up and exclaimed, "The truth of water as the truth of everything else is a wonderful wisdom, a knowledge and power ineffable, an infinite delight."

The Master smiled and spoke not, neither affirming nor negating. But the disciple understood through an inner contact. And others wondered and tried to fathom the meaning of the disciple's words and still more of the Master's rich and pregnant silence.

Sowing the Seed

The disciples wondered as to how the Master made the selection. Some of them appeared simply too ordinary and commonplace people to justify the Master's decision.

One day seeing one of them behave in an exceptionally rough manner, one of the disciples asked of the Master as to why he chose that kind of humanity.

The Master asked the disciple, "What makes you feel you are superior to him?"

The disciple saw through his mask of goodness and kept quiet. But another asked the question again.

The Master simply smiled and asked if it was easier to turn a virtuous man to God than one prone to sin and wrongdoing.

"Of course, the virtuous," the eager disciples answered.

"Not necessarily, perhaps even more difficult since the virtuous is often self-conceited. Satisfied with himself he does not feel the need to strive for anything higher while the wrong doer if he knows in his heart his weakness may be more ready since he is full of humility," answered the Master.

"But still, some seem to be incorrigible, what about that?" The Master laughed and jokingly responded, "So do you want or expect God to do easy things! Maybe He likes to take challenges and try out different things rather than follow a strict logical rule."

"But some hardly ever change," asked another who was restless and intolerant of others.

"Oh, and how do you judge that, my child? Each one finds his own difficulty big or is blind to it but is over observant of other's mistakes, often the mistakes that he hides within and fails to see in himself," the Master remonstrated.

"By their behaviour," one responded who could see nothing but the most external and outer aspects of life.

"Is that so?" the Master quizzed the disciple and then went on to explain how all authentic change appeared from within outward whereas the other type of change where men simply polish their exterior personality and behaviour without a corresponding inner change was an eyewash and hypocrisy.

He took them to a garden and showed how the bud discloses itself from within outwards and the plants grow from a tiny seed step by step and the tree trunk and branches renew themselves from within before they change on the outside and, sometimes, they may not even though the tree is constantly changing within. However, the artificial flowers and plants were ready-made and polished outside but were lifeless with no further possibility of growth within them.

The disciples began to understand a little of the Master's methods. "So, you sow the seeds and leave time and nature to do the rest and work out the details and bring the plant to fullness and flower and give fruits! Then why this selection?" asked one.

"Well, if the season is not right and the soil is not ready or the field unprepared for the harvest, would not the seed fail to come out? So also, is with human beings. If the inner nature is not ready or the circumstances too difficult, then sowing the seed prematurely only stifles it. To learn to wait is to put time on your side. A certain readiness of nature is required before the seed of divine life can be planted within it." So saying the

Master moved on even as the disciples wondered at his strange yet natural ways.

How Many Paths

The Master had trod many ways. A disciple asked him once as to how many spiritual paths were there.

"As many as there are human beings," replied the Master rather laconically, and then added after a pause, "there are as many paths as there are aspiring souls and yet in reality there is only one path."

"And which path is that?" asked one who had a special liking for a particular way hoping to get the approval of his methods.

But the Master responded rather quizzically, "Well, it is the path that is no path!"

Seeing the puzzled look on the faces of the disciples he explained by taking them to the seashore where the sun was just beginning to rise and its first reflections fell upon the waters. A small section of the sea was lit up by the sun as its rays fell upon it. He asked one of them if he saw a path of light over the waters.

"Yes, of course, right in front of me," the eager disciple noted.

Requesting him to stay there, the Master took a few steps further and asked another disciple if he also saw a path of light upon the sea in front of him.

"Yes, of course, it is there right in front," said the second. And so on and so forth. As they moved ahead, each one noted a path of light upon the sea right in front, irrespective of how far they went.

"There you are," said the Master, "see how the one path becomes many depending upon the angle of your vision, the starting point of your journey, the route you take and the goal you set in front of you. In fact, there is only one path and that is the universal path of the sun. With its help we climb to the Light and Force that governs the world. It is the sunlit path. But men are not yet wide and their vision too narrow, so they break the path into several streams and oppose it to each other."

What Humanity Really Needs

The Master had the deepest love and compassion for the struggling soul of man upon earth but his compassion was not blinded and he seldom seemed to encourage acts of charity and philanthropy of the kind practised by rich men. He neither discouraged nor encouraged it. But in general, he observed that it had little to do with true spiritual growth and did not want people to confuse one for the other.

On being asked he would simply reply, "What does humanity need most, food and comfort for the body or release from the bondage of Ignorance by the growing Light of his soul?"

When questioned whether a poor man can think of God, he would laugh and say with the ring of experience that it is often the poor whose hearts are more open to God than the rich ones. Too much money was not necessarily a sign of some special Grace. Rather it was often a curse, for it put the man into so many traps and bonds that made it even more difficult to break than if he were less privileged materially. He agreed that spirituality had little do with riches or poverty and a rich man as well as a poor may be deeply spiritual if they have arrived at the inner readiness. It only made it more difficult for the rich to turn to God.

"So should one discard one's wealth if it comes in the way of our spiritual progress?"

"How about using it divinely?" the Master would say. "It is easier to discard a difficulty rather than transform it and turn it into an opportunity to serve God's purpose in the world. If God has given us wealth, we should turn it for the good of the world, but not through blind pity but as guided by the Divine Vision."

"By distributing it to the poor?" asked one unable to get the true import of the Master's statement.

"No that is the worst way since it would encourage lethargy and stifle the heart and soul of another who receives money as charity. The wealth that is received without any effort often leads to its misuse except in the rare few." the Master replied.

"So should one build hospitals and schools for free and for the poor?" asked another.

"And increase diseases and the ills that modern education brings with its almost exclusive emphasis on man as a biological entity whose only goal is to survive!" quipped the Master. He went on to add, "There is no use repeating the past follies blindly. What humanity needs most is a new vision in the mind, a new hope and faith in his heart, a new impulse and will to live for greater aims and deeper goals. Instead of opening hospitals and multiplying diseases why not find out the root cause of human maladies and the master remedy. We need educational institutions that can embody the new Light."

"But that is a vision," complained another. "How can I use my wealth to further a vision?" he asked.

"Surely wealth will not give you the new vision for that can only come through personal growth," the Master responded. "But if you have sympathy for the new vision and one has wealth then it can be put at its service. For, to express this new vision upon earth and reach it out to the many who are still blind, you need both, men of vision who can carry it afar and also men of action to organize it. So also, you need men of wealth to create new institutions and support old ones that would embody this new Light. That indeed is the best service that one can render for earth through wealth."

A rich man proud of his philanthropy asked what the Master thought about those rich people who spent a lot of money on charity.

The Master had a hearty laugh and remarked, "It is often like the case of a robber sharing a little of his loot with those whom he has looted and thereby assuage his guilt and flatter his ego." But then not wanting to disappoint the man he added, "Well, if a rich man wants to distribute money or open hospitals, that is his business and if he has nothing more to give and no other vision to uphold, then let him do that especially if that is his calling. But he should not think that he is doing something very great to solve the problem of humanity or what he is doing is greater than the poor man who is quietly seeking God in his hermitage."

"But don't the hermitage and the ashrams also need money? And is it not a waste of life for a young man to spend the prime of his youth doing nothing except seeking God and live on the wealth of others when he could earn that wealth for himself and be independent," asked the rich man again unwilling to give up.

"And what makes you feel that the young man seeking God is doing nothing. Try doing it and you will understand that it is far more difficult to seek God than to earn bags full of money," the Master calmly replied.

The rich man would not concede, "But why should others support his quest, to whose benefit is it when he could easily earn for himself?"

The Master became serious on seeing the degree of human resistance to Light. He responded, "The young man seeking God is doing a great benefit to the society. Firstly, he is earning spiritual wealth that the others are not ready to earn. Once he earns it, he shares this inner wealth with others as the great Masters and their erstwhile disciples do. In fact, their gift is much more than the money that you give for their needs. You look after their physical needs while they look after your spiritual needs. So, who is the gainer?"

"But such disciples and such masters are few and far between, what about the others? Are they not parasites upon society?" he argued one last time.

"On the contrary, even the failures in the spiritual path do a service to mankind for they at least keep the fire of the soul alive by their sheer effort. And when even one succeeds, he makes it easier for many others to follow. Even if he does not speak about it his mere presence brings the earth in contact with forces of Harmony, Peace and Light. He is like a silent dynamo that energizes the earth and rejuvenates its sick body by digging out from our nature's deep streams that soothe and heal man's mind, heart and soul. They are like beacon Lights, if not Lighthouses, for the man to follow on the dangerous roads of destiny to the great discovery that awaits us all one day. The seeker of Light is the spearhead in this eternal collective quest of mankind who makes the way for others to follow and even if he falls, he becomes a brick to bridge the way towards the future. Do you then still feel with the superficial thinkers that the spiritual man is simply a do-nothing or is it simply that his great contribution goes unnoticed and he cares little for it either."

The words of the Master fell upon listening ears and the earth suddenly woke up to fresh and sublime memories that stirred in its silent deeps, memories of spiritual heroes and martyrs whose life was a burning example and without whom this world would long have sunk to perdition or gone to blazes.

The Birth and Death of Suffering and Sin

The Master was taking a stroll in the garden. The group of disciples surrounded him like bees around a flower that had turned the light and power of the sun into a sweet and strengthening nectar for their thirsty struggling souls.

Feeling the mood of the moment, one among them asked as to how come in this world of beauty there came to dwell evil and suffering. The Master became pensive and took them to a nearby place where the gardener had just thrown some seeds into the ground. Pointing to the soil and the seed below it, he asked them why should the seed of the beautiful flower, destined to partake of the sun, be put underneath the soil into a dark space and breath the waste and the mire and rot on the surface and struggle to reach the top against the heavy resistance of the earth.

"To throw its roots deep," said one. "To cast off its hard shell," replied another.

The Master smiled and exclaimed, "That's the answer to your question. Suffering is like the waste and the mire and Evil like the darkness and the resistance that man's soul must face so that it can also throw its roots deep into the earth and its surface crust softens in due time. The surface crust is the ego-self, the source of all evil and suffering, When the inner being is ready by the pressure of the world forces, when it has cast its roots deep and strong, then the ego-self slowly dissolves and the deeper soul emerges into Light and Freedom. It is delivered out of the womb of darkness and is ready for a new adventure into Light and its climb towards the sun. But if the seed is stripped bare of its hard crust prematurely and exposed too early to the light of the sun and the immense freedom of space then it may simply burn off and be blown away by the strong winds before its roots have steadied it. So also what we call error, evil and suffering are simply necessary intermediary steps and stages in man's ascending growth towards Light and Freedom."

"What then is sin and what then is a virtue?" enquired another.

The Master observed, as he moved from one flowering tree to another, "Look at the buds, their petals closed upon each other, their fragrance trapped inside. That is the first stage of the flower. It is as if it is trying not only to feel and hold but also to capture and possess the light it so badly needs and to keep the fragrance to its solitary self that is meant to be its gift to the world. So also, is with man. Selfishness is the only sin since it induces man to try and appropriate things for his solitary self and give out nothing in return to the world. The result is that it remains dark inside and closed outside. But a time comes when the bud begins to trust the Light that it feels and opens out to it and all that surrounds it in a spontaneous gesture of self-giving. And, lo and behold, its self-giving is instantly rewarded by the fullness of its bloom and its generous uncalculating gift of fragrance turns into sweet nectar inside. Man is selfish in his early stages of growth but soon he must realise that selfishness is a trap since it prevents him from getting the very thing that he most needs and wants. With this awakening and the pressure of Light and its own secret nature there comes in him the trust and the confidence to open out and give itself first to the world around it which alone he sees with his half-open eyes and then to the sun that he begins to perceive as his eternal source, the secret master of his journey, the fosterer who turns all things to honey within him. Then man becomes a link between the earth and the heaven." Then with a mystic pause, he added, "Selfishness too, that origin of all sin, is a preliminary stage in human growth. This too must pass away as the man begins to trust God within and His play around and gives himself freely to both or rather to God and His play in the world."

The Master sat down quietly on a little rocky promontory in the garden, his gaze as if fixed into infinity, his look encompassing the whole of space in a single glance, his heart one with all things in their eternal essence. And the disciples sat around him wondering whom to admire, the sweet fragrance of the flowers that gave themselves generously to everything around them or the earth that shared the joy, the struggle and the sorrow of all things giving shelter and place to each thing that must wait for its season to turn ripe and to blossom emerging out of the darkness into the Light, or the sun that gave itself to the creation and though far and high, beyond the reach of earth and its creatures, yet was the secret source and support of all. And as they thus contemplated their inner and outer gaze was fixed upon the Master who was to earth and men, at once the flower and the earth and the sun.

The Egg and the Chick

The young aspirants were full of enthusiasm to spread the gospel of their Master. Was it not the best way for them to express their gratitude to Him who had shown them the Light? But the Master generally discouraged this. He would often say that Truth needs no advertisements and the sun needs none to announce its coming to the world. He would tell them jocularly that the crow and the cock remain the same even though they are among the first ones to feel the coming of the sun and wake up the entire neighbourhood with their cries.

"But is it not our duty to announce to the world the truth that we have known?" asked a few.

"Yes, you must share the joy of your discovery. But a reading of it or even hearing of it is not enough," said the Master, and added, "first hear, then think and meditate till you can see and realize it in yourself. That is knowing."

A few persisted. The Master left them free to discover the truth of His words in their own way. For this was His method. He would suggest but never impose, counsel but never order. He left each one free to follow his own nature and led each according to their law of inner growth.

Some felt confused at this. Their small minds wanted a narrow rigid doctrine applicable to all. The Master would explain how such a thing would soon turn the truth of His words into a narrow sect and a religion. For the Divine does not act according to a fixed principle or dogma but in infinite freedom and liberty. His is not a dictatorial kingdom where all be compelled to obey Him. That would make a truly mechanical world of men who are more like robots than living and thinking creatures. God lives in freedom and gives this freedom to all as the first condition of growth.

"But is this freedom not dangerous when we do not know what is good and what is bad for us?" asked someone who was a strict disciplinarian by nature. But the Master simply smiled and said, "Perhaps, but how else can there be authentic growth without the direct experience of things? And as of danger, did I not create them for man to overcome them and grow stronger through the difficulties! Man fears danger and is afraid of error and thereby man also limits his perfection. But God allies with evil and sin to bring light and good and makes our errors the steppingstones upon the heavenward way."

One among them who felt himself holier than others lamented as he observed how this freedom had spoilt the disciples. He mused under his breath if there was any difference at all between the life of the aspirants here and the life of ordinary men.

And the Master heard his unspoken thought and felt the disciple's ego of holiness heave under his holy breast even as He spoke, "Be not deceived by appearances. Some sticks that seem straight outside are crooked below the water. Others that appear twisted and kinked at several places are so because they have entwined their life around the vast and complex body of the tree of Truth. Unable to clasp it they have thus entwined themselves around It and thereby appear crooked. Yet are they centred around Truth in their inner being!"

"But sometimes we find no difference between some of us here and those who are outside leading an ordinary life. Is this too a deception of the eyes or is there a difference?" asked another, unable to fathom the diverse ways of the Master who dealt differently with each one, often defying a simple understanding based on standard norms and conventions.

"Of course, there is a difference. It is like the difference between the fertilized and the unfertilized egg. To all outer appearances, they may look alike for a long time with common virtues and vices. But to an inward eye, they are different. The aspirant however is like a fertilized egg in whom the seed of divinity has been cast. His inner being begins to get shaped by the power within it even though the outer nature may appear the same as anyone else. Then a time comes when all is ripe and something breaks free from within the fertilized egg and the chick is born. The soul force is released. The resistances and barriers of the outer nature break under its growing pressure. But the unfertilized egg has been delivered prematurely. It remains the same until it is swallowed by the cosmic powers and dies to itself."

And as a word of caution to their premature enthusiasm he added: "While the highest possibility of an unfertilized egg is to provide nourishment to another by its own destruction, the fertilized egg must avoid this. Its destiny is fulfilled by going under the brooding wings of the Divine Grace and waiting with patience, letting the new thing develop within. The heat of the Divine Tapas then prepares the chick and one day sets it free to grow into the likeness of its creator. Only then are they ready to go into the world and mingle amidst ordinary life and carry the seeds of Fire and Light that the Divine has put in them to places far and wide.

The Nectar of Immortality

The Master sat under the cool shade of the Banyan tree. A little below him gathered around his presence young and old disciples, swift and brilliant in thought, energetic and full of enthusiasm, glad in heart and calm in speech and countenance; they sat around their Master as the ministers gather around a king. But this was a king whose slightest wish was their command and to obey him their soul's right and privilege.

So they gathered late in the noon after the chores of the ashrama were over, expectant and eager for the nectar drops that would flow out of the Master's heart in the form of stories from a hoary past. The Master's touch turned these well-known or unknown tales into keys to unlock an inner door that opens upon the pathway towards the future.

A disciple started the conversation, "Tell us, dear Master, the story of that great endeavour when the gods and the titans came together?"

"You mean the tale about the churning of the ocean and the nectar of immortality?" asked the Master. The disciple nodded with a smile of approval.

The Master started, his gaze looking far upon the horizon as he was travelling far back in Time or perhaps into another Time-Space Dimension, for indeed the story is of another dimension, a fourth dimension beyond our earthly sense, yet whatever happens there casts its influence upon the earth. So, the Master told the tale as follows:

"The gods and the titans are ever at war. The gods have wisdom but not as much strength. They can give wisdom, they also have compassion but when it comes to force, it is the titans who have an upper hand."

"Naturally, the titans have the upper hand in the battle using all means to win, being fierce and cruel by nature."

"The gods did not know what to do. Their defeat or even retreat meant that the demoniac qualities would grow on earth and human hearts would become hard and given only to lust and greed. So they approached the great god, Vishnu, the preserver who dwells as Narayana in the human heart. Vishnu gave audience to the gods. Their concern was his concern as well. For the defeat of gods meant a diminution of godlike qualities and that would mean a great disorder."

The disciples' faces began to beam as they began to see a new sense in the story, a meaning that was relevant to them.

The Master continued:

"Narayana, the all-pervading Godhead who has chosen to dwell in the human heart so that men may not stray far away from dharma, spoke thus to the gods, 'The titans are stronger and cruel as well. You, the gods, are wise and compassionate. Through wisdom, you have learnt humility and surrender therefore have you come to me for help. I will surely help you. But first, you must find the nectar of immortality. It is that which will make you strong and invincible against the titans.'"

"A smile of secrecy lingered upon the great Lord's lips. And the gods looking at each other with amazement and wonder asked, 'The nectar of immortality. But where can we find it, Lord?'"

"The gracious Lord continued, 'You will find it in the deepest depths of the ocean of knowledge, Ksheera Sagar, that upholds the great world-serpent, Time, whose uncoiling carries the world–march forward and in whose heart, I, the guardian of the law, am asleep.'

"There was a moment's pause yet a pause in which one felt as if ages passed away, for a moment of the Lord is a thousand years of earthly life. The Lord resumed:

'In the depths of this ocean of knowledge lies the nectar of immortality born out Bliss that is at the core of everything. But you cannot reach it by your wisdom alone; you also need the strength of the titans. If both the sides, the gods and the titans, come together and churn this ocean, you will receive the nectar of immortality as your portion and having that you would become invincible.'

"'But won't the titans too have it and become immortal and invincible,' the gods expressed genuine concern."

"The gracious Lord smiled reassuringly, 'Leave that to me for eventually the titans and the gods both but obey the law of their nature. And unless the titans change themselves, they will be unable to have a portion of the nectar. Even after the long and difficult labour of the churning, there is the last test that would stand as a veil between them and the nectar, a veil they are unable to tear for they have not the knowledge.'"

"The gods started to return full of renewed hope. As they were preparing to go back to their world, the great Lord cautioned them, 'But remember, before the nectar comes out, there will emerge out of this ocean, the deadliest of all poisons, kalakuta. Be not frightened for it must be thrown out as a preliminary purification before the nectar comes.' He added, 'And see that you covet nothing, let the Asuras have what they want for many beautiful gifts will emerge out of the churning. You keep your eyes fixed upon your goal, the nectar of immortality.'"

The Master paused for a moment and throwing a meaningful glance at the disciples added, "The gods returned full of hope and joy for that is the effect of the Lord's presence and his reassurance."

He continued as the disciples were all in rapt attention, "So the gods returned rejoicing. They also sent an emissary to the titans with a proposal for the joint venture of churning the ocean of knowledge for the nectar of immortality. The titans agreed after much discussion and debate. The two groups gathered near the ocean, the titans led by king Bali (a name that symbolizes strength) and the gods led by Indra (a name that symbolizes knowledge surpassing the senses). The mountain Mandara, (the embodiment of material consciousness) was placed at the centre of the ocean. Vasuki, the great serpent who represents the energy that labours in darkness at the root of the world, consented to become the rope that would be tied around the great mount. To prevent the mountain from sinking into the ocean, God Himself became a grant tortoise, kurmavatara, and held the mountain on his back."

"Now the great effort began. To initiate the process, The Lord himself held Vasuki towards its mouth. The gods followed him as they always did. But the jealous Asuras took it as a prestige issue. Vain and ambitious, they wanted to be honoured first. So, they raised a hue and cry against the gods holding the mouth of the serpent Vasuki. The gods readily conceded and moved over to the tail–side. Little did the titans realise that Narayana, the Lord was being gracious towards them by holding the mouth. For as the churning proceeded the breath of the great serpent phew out poisonous fumes. But that turned out to be nothing compared to what was to come."

"As the churning went on, suddenly, the air became full of stifling poison. So deadly was its effect that both the gods and the titans began to run helter-skelter to escape the poison. This indeed was *Halahal*, the bitterness and darkness buried in the subconscient parts of our nature. We must confront this one day and only after we are purged free of it that the gifts of the spirit can emerge."

"But now, the poison threatened everything. What could be done? The air was full of anxiety and fear. But the great Lord smiled reassuringly and at his behest, there appeared on the horizons, the deathless Shiva, the eternal who takes back all things into him, for out of him they are born. In a mighty gesture of great compassion, Shiva took the whole poison in the hollow of his palm and drank it. Only a drop was left for the earth to bear. The rest stained his throat and thus, was he named 'Neelkantha', the poison–stain only enhancing his beauty and greatness."

"The threat of the bitterest poison being over, the churning continued. Now it was the turn of the various gifts to emerge, the winged horse, Ucchaisravas, that Bali, the titan king, took away; Airavata, the snow-white seven tusked elephant that was given to the king of gods, Indra. Then there was the Jewel, Kaustubh mani, that adorned Narayana's chest and Lakshmi of unparalleled beauty, charm and grace whom none deserved. She chose Lord Vishnu, the purest of all as her Lord and consort. At last came Varuni, with intoxicating eyes evoking desire in all. The titans wanted and received her."

The Master paused for a while, as a disciple interrupted, "But what are these gifts, the flying horse, the seven–tusked elephant, are these not mere imaginations and myths, surely they do not exist?" The disciple looked puzzled as the Master resumed with a smile on his face, "And Kamdhenu, the cow who could grant any wish was given to the seers, engaged in various *tapasyas*, I forgot to mention her."

The disciple interrupted again as if something flashed across his mind's sky as a revelation, "Oh, I see, is that why you are able to grant our wishes? So the cow is the symbol of plenty."

The Master smiled again, "Surely, not all wishes, for that will not be a wise thing to do. Granting all wishes may sometimes lead only to an increase of desire, laziness and even vanity. That is why she is given to the rishis who have mastered the art of self-control. The cow itself is a Vedic symbol for Light of knowledge, just as the horse is a symbol of force and elephant a symbol of prosperity and quiet strength. So, now you can see the truth behind the symbol."

"Nevertheless, to resume the last and the most interesting part of the story, finally, and at last, there emerged the most handsome being, healthy and beautiful in every way, full of youthful energies, Dhanvantari, dressed in a light with a golden hue, carrying in both his hands a crystal bowl with a golden light around it. In that cup, there was concealed the most coveted of all boons, the nectar of immortality."

"Now, as Dhanvantari appeared with the nectar, there was great jubilation around. But as they say, the real test, of character is when we are faced with the extremes of success or failure. Seeing the nectar, the titans completely forgot the joint venture and the pact. They rushed and, as is their nature, snatched the bowl by force and ran away to drink it themselves. But soon a fight ensued amongst themselves over who would be the first recipient. The gods watched all this with dismay and stunned as they were, and as is consistent with their nature, they turned to the great Lord with submission and prayer for help. The gracious Lord who is in all things, who has become the strength of the titans and the light of the gods, simply spread out his hand in a gesture of reassurance and vanished from their vision. They waited with hope and trust."

"Meanwhile, the infighting amongst the titans continued. Being sons of darkness and division, they are ever quarrelling even between themselves. But as they were thus trying to snatch the bowl from the hands of each other, there appeared on the threshold of their sight, a form most beautiful to behold. A woman of endless charm appeared amidst them and the titans were as if hypnotized by her presence."

"'Who are you, O! Loveliest and fairest of all who beats all that we have seen or heard of until now?' the titans inquired."

"And the woman with a smile for which the triple worlds would be an easy price to pay said, 'I am Viswa-Mohini, the most charming form that ever was made.'"

"'Would you then do this for us?' the titans asked entrusting the bowl and the nectar in her hand, 'Would you distribute it to us? We will abide by whatever you decide.'"

"'Are you sure?' the charming woman sought to confirm, 'The sages say that you must be careful in entrusting yourself to charming appearances.'"

"But the Titans were already blinded. Smitten by greed and lust, they joined in a burst of hideous laughter, 'Ho, ho! The sages, who cares for what they say? They keep telling everyone to deny the very things that would give happiness, wealth, wine and woman. Ha, ha, ha! The sages, forget what they say, we will accept whatever, you decide for us.'"

"Lust had blinded their eyes and arrogance had fanned their vanity and false self-confidence."

"The woman did not insist. She asked the titans to be seated to the left and the gods to the right. And as she passed in between the two rows, she kept pouring a bewitching smile to the titans and the nectar to the gods. The titans were still too dazed to take notice except one, Rahu, who saw the trick and changed sides. But even before he could drink the nectar, the woman changed her form and assuming the form of the great god Vishnu, cut off his head with the luminous discus, Sudarshana Chakra. But a drop had gone to the throat and Rahu's head became immortal, a queer creature, half-titan and half-god, born out of a crucial last moment choice."

"The titans felt cheated and rushed with all their force upon the gods who now, rejuvenated by the nectar, gave a good fight and sent them packing, back to their heels."

"Frustrated, the titans returned, blaming the great god Vishnu and preparing themselves for another fight."

"But the god within their hearts smiled. For truly they stood cheated by their own lustful and greedy nature. For such is the decree given of old!"

"They who abandon desire
Shall find the delight they seek through things
They who pursue and possess shall lose,
For such is the law given the man by the sages
To all claimants of immortality
A difficult task is this,
A labour dual and fierce
At the end of which
There still awaits a tremendous choice,
What do you seek for the nectar of delight
   the cup of immortality?
If for thy ego, then thou must still wait.
But if for the growth of goodness, light and love
   in earth and men
Then thou shalt strive rightly
And seek and possess."

The Master had summed it up so beautifully. The lights were slowly falling low as the sunset was in sight. But the inner light had grown within the disciples, their sight widened to greater horizons.

They slowly got up from their seats. It was time to light the fire.

The Dwarf with Three Strides

Once again, the disciples had gathered under the cool shade of the banyan tree. The Master arrived as usual at the appointed time. It was not in his nature to make others wait for him, even if they were his disciples. The story session began with a discussion over the story of *Amrita-Manthan* which the disciples had heard before.

Disciple: "Master, you narrated the story of Amrita-Manthan the other day and it appeared perfectly natural that the Lord distributed the nectar to the gods while denying it to the titans. But hadn't they too laboured for it and therefore deserved it equally? Then why was the Lord partial to the gods?"

The Master seemed to be waiting for this question. He responded at once, "But the Lord was not being partial at all though it may seem so to the human eye. He was simply doing what ought to be done as the right thing." Then after a pause, he added, "well, he was rendering Divine Justice, if you like?"

"Divine Justice," a few disciples exclaimed as if puzzled for they had never thought that there could be several kinds of justice.

The Master resumed, "Yes, each earthly value, whether Love, Charity, Kindness, Unity, Justice has its divine and a human counterpart. The Divine renders Justice as per the Divine vision which is a complete vision and a total knowledge. He sees not only the outer effort but also the inner motives, the hidden forces at play, the long-term results and above all the good of the earth. Even when he destroys, he destroys out of love. Man sees only the surface of things and has at most only a brief life's vision, therefore, is he perplexed and confused at the ways of God. True, the titans laboured as fiercely and perhaps even more than the gods, but their motives were unclear. Had the nectar been given to them, that would have spelt disaster for earth and humanity on whom these beings of other dimensions cast their influence. Have you not heard what Sri Krishna has said in the Gita about the right course of action, dharma? This right, from the Divine point of view, is what helps in the evolutionary march of mankind towards the ultimate Truth and Light. Have you not heard of the Lord's incarnations as the dwarf child, Vamana avatara?"

One of the disciples inquired, "Tell us, Master, the story of Vamana. I have heard about it as a child but couldn't quite grasp the sense behind it."

The disciples were all attention, expectantly waiting for another story. The Master got into the frame of telling another story, of another incarnation. As he spoke, a joy flowed from his body as if he experienced what he recounted:

"The titan king Bali had not forgotten his defeat. He performed various forms of austerities to gain rare weapons. Then, armoured with these and gathering around himself a huge army, he marched towards Amravati, the city of deathless gods where Indra resides. Seeing the huge army and the rare weapons, Indra in consultation with the guru of gods, Brihaspati, decided to abandon the city and go into a hideout with the rest of the gods. Better be free even with nothing than be a slave to the titans which seemed imminent. Brihaspati, who knows the ways of the Vast, explained to Indra, the king of gods, thus: 'After God's will, one must respect Time for it is through the agency of Time that the great Lord works and acts. He who acts completely ignoring the conditions set forth by Time in this huge cosmic play brings only doom to oneself. For in all things, Time works. There is a Time for victory, there is a Time also for defeat. And he who knows how to accept both success and failure with grace and dignity, eventually masters Time itself.'"

"Brihaspati spoke, but Indra was still not fully convinced. The gods are not powerless, he thought. Why should we not fight? But Brihaspati, the wise said, 'Look Indra, the time is not good right now for your victory. The Lord, in his mysterious way, has brought you face to face with inevitable defeat. Perhaps he wants you and the gods to learn the lesson of humility. However powerful you may be, Time over-rides and overtops all things. So concede right now to avoid destruction of this beautiful city and its many inhabitants.'"

"Indra listened, for the gods always obeyed their guru. Along with the other gods, he took refuge in devmata Aditi's home. Aditi, the Mother of the gods, received them with Love and Compassion that is always there in her heart for all her children. The gods forgot all their pain and humiliations in Her presence as the ever kind mother carried the sorrow and anguish of the gods to the great Lord, Narayana, 'Wherefore this ignominy, defeat and humiliation for my radiant children. Lord, you must intervene on their behalf for their kingdom has been snatched unjustly by the titans.'"

"The gracious Lord smiled and reassured Aditi, the mother of the gods: 'What thou hast willed for them, I cannot refuse. It is granted. The kingdom of the gods will be returned to them in due course of time, for as thou knowest, my will is executed by the trustee, Time. The heavens have been snatched from the gods without a fight, for the gods had to learn a lesson. It is Time and not the titan king who snatched it away. And it is Time who shall give it back to them without a fight.'"

"Thus, assured the mother of the gods who mediates between the anguish of the gods and the ecstasies of the highest Being, returned and resumed her work of nurturing and strengthening the gods, pouring her Grace and Love upon them, healing all their anguish and sorrow."

"Time rolled by. Meanwhile, a little child with an unusual radiance was born to Aditi. He emerged out of her womb, a radiant god himself whose splendour was greater even than that of Indra, the king of gods. The earth, the moon, the sun, the fire, the mother goddess Parvati herself, Brahma and Shiva all gave something of their aspect of energies to him. His form resembled Narayana himself and Aditi knew that the Time had come for the gods to get back their due. The little boy, well versed in the Veda, remained dwarf-bodied, Vamana, but in his consciousness, he was vaster than the skies and deeper than the oceans."

"Meanwhile, king Bali who was now commanding the three worlds, the physical material world, the subtle world built of prana and the still subtler world of mind, decided to perform a rare yajna that would make him invincible. The yajna was being presided over by the guru of the titans, Shukracharya. As a master of all the elemental forces and material energies, Shukracharya wanted the titans to become invincible. As he thus proceeded on the yajna, suddenly a dazzling radiance was seen approaching near the sacrificial fire.

"The titans were perplexed for they were not accustomed to so much light. Some even fainted unable to bear the effulgence which, as it neared, was seen to be emanating from Vamana who was approaching the Yajnasala dressed in the barest of bare clothes, he held a Kamandalu in his hands and an umbrella made of reeds over his head. His eyes were full of an unearthly joy and the countenance full of peace and radiance. A beautiful fragrance of jasmine emanated from his body that had a lotus pink hue around it. As he approached the Yajnasala, the titan king was filled with a strange joy. Indeed, he thought the little boy to be the fire god himself. Offering his obeisance to the young bright Brahmin boy, the titan king asked him: 'Who art thou, O young one? You seem to be a celestial being or perhaps the Lord himself in a miniature form. Tell me what can be offered to you as a due share of the yajna?'"

At this, the Master paused and elaborated a little about the yajna: "Yajna is not merely an external rite as some see it. In principle, it is a recognition of the fact that we are neither alone nor the only ones in the universe. Through yajna, the sacrificant offered what he had and what he could, to others, to men of wisdom and valour, to men in need, to the subjects in one's kingdom, to the gods and denizens of other worlds. The fire is the inner fire, the eternal witness, the Divine will in man. Through that as one's witness, one makes the offering. But this is not a one-way process, for, in return, the elements, the earth, the sun, the moon, the sea, the gods also gave to the giver something of their forces and their energies. Thus, each could grow into the All and the Whole"

The disciples were amazed at the depth and profundity of this ancient wisdom that they not only saw oneness behind all things but also provided a way to realize it through yajna, as one of the powerful means.

The Master resumed: "To come back to our story, the radiant Vamana thus spoke to the titan king, 'O great king, you are truly generous and large-hearted, much like your father and grandfather. All that I need, however, is just three steps worth of land.'"

"Now, Vamana knew that the titans are readily carried away by praise. They are generous but their generosity is driven by the ego and displayed for the sake of self-flattery. Bali too felt flattered but was also somewhat surprised at the small measure of the gift. He asked the little dwarf to reconsider and ask for more. But Vamana, the dwarf stood his ground."

"Meanwhile, as the two were conversing, Shukracharya had perceived that this was no ordinary being and his measure need not be our measure. He advised the titan king not to grant what Vamana had asked for as there may be some trick behind it. But the titan king would not listen. He was full of vanity and boastfulness. 'What trick can this little dwarf do with me, Bali, who rules the three worlds and of whom even the gods are afraid of? If I listen to my guru, I may bring shame to my family pride who were known to be generous kings. What will people speak of me, that the mighty king Bali did not keep his promise for mere three steps of land?' He thought, 'My guru has lost his senses to thus advise me. I know better,' and thus, with the fire as a witness and the water as the sanctifier, he promised Vamana to take three steps worth of space anywhere in the three worlds."

"And Vamana smiled. He took one step and his being seemed to tower to unimaginable heights. With his first step, he measured the entire earth. His second step covered the heavens and all else in-between. The titan king was all amazed. Realizing that Vamana was none else but Narayana himself, he stood with folded hands, speechless and in wonder."

"'Where do I place my third step, O! great and generous king?' He heard Vamana's sweet and soft voice that was like celestial music to his ears."

"Still held almost in trance, the king bowed his head and gestured that the third step may be placed thereupon his head. This gesture meant that his ego may be completely demolished and his whole being reclaimed by the Lord himself."

"Vamana, the Lord who had assumed the stature of a dwarf smiled as he granted Bali the highest boon possible, by taking away the burden of ego, pride and vanity that man carries on his head."

"'O! Great and noble king, the earth and the heavens were already mine. I have only reclaimed them from you who thought that they were yours. I give them now to the gods to govern and to you, I give the highest of the nether worlds, Sutala where you will reign a while as my trustee. In return for your noble gesture, I promise that I will always be by your side, even in the nether worlds, for there is nothing small or dark where I cannot reside and even in the darkest, mysterious and the fallen worlds, I am there, hidden and masked. Now that you have chosen to surrender your ego to Me, I shall quickly purify your nature and after this cycle of creation withdraws, it is you whom I shall appoint as the guardian of heaven, the king of gods, Indra, for the next cycle.'"

"And Bali bowed his head in utter gratitude as the Lord placed his feet over his head and sent him to the nether worlds."

The Master paused for a while as in deep contemplation. Then addressing his disciples, he asked, "What would you call this—Divine Justice or Divine Compassion, Retribution or Reward, taking or giving, disgrace or the greatest Grace?"

The disciples were unable to answer.

The Master resumed, "For such is the wisdom that has built the world. Justice and injustice, these are human terms, needed for us, but the Lord sees and act differently and does what is needed for our growth."

The evening was spreading fast. The Master summarized, revealing the symbol of the story, "Vamana, the radiant portion, *amsa* of the Lord is man's soul, his psychic being, dwarf in appearance but formidable in power and knowledge.

So long as the ego is battling out between the 'good' and the 'bad', the 'bright' and the 'dark' side of life, Vamana remains hidden from our sight. But a time comes when we are ready through suffering and humility, when the world—mother Aditi, intercedes on our behalf and Vamana, the soul in man emerges out of Her and begins to spread its radiance and influence upon our life. He reclaims our nature for the Lord to whom everything belongs. And when we have offered our ego to him, He purifies us quickly and abides with us always wherever we are. Then sin and evil fall away from us and, whether in hell or in heaven, we become radiant instruments of God."

The Master fell silent but, the disciples felt a strange joy and peace invade their hearts and an urge to give themselves utterly and entirely to the Lord. Quietly, they stood up, one after another and walked for the last errands. It was night outside but inside all was light, happiness and peace.

The Soul's Dwelling Place

The disciple entered and found the Master cleaning the room. A little embarrassed, he rushed forward and offered help, "Oh, Master, please let me do this."

The Master smiled while continuing to clean, "But this is nothing compared to the cleaning that I do every day in countless rooms of each one."

A little quizzically, the disciple stood wondering at the deep import of the Master's words. By now the work at hand was over. The Master gently kept the cleaning cloth aside, neatly folded as if it was his way of expressing love and gratitude towards the little objects that served him. How much care he bestowed on everyone and everything, men and physical objects, animals and plants and who knows the gods and demons alike as if He saw the indivisible unity of all things. There was nothing big or small in his eyes, nothing trivial and merely mundane.

By now the disciples had gathered around him returning from their respective workplaces. Just as cows return home from their pasture, these souls had flocked around the Master for the deeper nourishment of their famished souls.

As the Master settled in his chair, the disciple prompted, "Master, you were speaking about cleaning the rooms."

With a faint smile curved upon his beautiful lips, the Master responded: "Oh, that! Men spend so much time and energy in procuring food and lodging for their bodies but do very little for nourishing their souls or cleaning the house in which their soul dwells."

A brief pause followed. And the Master added: "All the values here are in an inverse order as if this world were an inverted image of God."

"What house is this that you speak of Master, pray enlighten us?" asked one as if asking the obvious.

The Master said, "This bodily house in which the soul dwells."

"But is not everyone busy taking care of this bodily house all the time," asked another.

"Do we?" The Master countered. "We do not take care of this bodily house in which the soul dwells. We rather spoil it through excess preoccupations, anxiety and fear on one hand and through excess of thrill, pleasure and comfort on the other. You see this house is not built by matter alone. Nature has tried and tested a million forms over millions of years before she could build this form in which the gods consented to dwell and through which we could once again discover God."

"Oh yes, there is that story in one of the Upanishads that speaks of the gods consenting to enter the human body. But we thought it is just a fable." One among them wondered.

"Not just a fable but a deep psycho-spiritual truth. The gods are powers and aspects of the Divine. Their willingness to enter the human body means that they are willing and ready to express their powers and forces through this bodily instrument and to fashion it towards a higher perfection." The Master responded. And then, a little pensively observed, "How soon do we spoil this wonderful instrument through wrong habits, wrong indulgences, wrong suggestions, through excesses and immoderations of every kind, through wrong thoughts, wrong feelings, wrong impulses, and wrong will."

One with a traditional background asked, "By wrong, you mean moral sins, isn't it Master?"

The Master answered, a little to their astonishment, "No, for one can be moral and follow all the rules of living and yet he may not care for his house."

"What does that mean, Master?" The discipline looked surprised. "If one leads a totally controlled and regulated bodily life and does not allow the body any form of immoral appetites, then is that not enough?"

"No, my child, it is not enough, for still he may live for the ego and the house may be given for the purposes of his selfish motives and not for the soul to dwell in it." Spoke the Master who had seen through the dualities of nature as well as the unity behind all things.

Then after a pause, he added revealing new horizons of thought and sight, "As I said this body is not built by matter alone. And what is matter itself but a condensation of the spirit. We are all made of a spiritual substance. The flesh is nothing else but Spirit concretized." The Master kept quiet for a moment while the disciples pondered, so accustomed were they to the idea of Spirit and matter as being opposed and antagonistic. Did they hear the Master right?

"We don't quite understand!" exclaimed one, while the other demurred "We always thought that the body was a trap and a deceit, a useless garment that must be discarded as soon as possible like a worn-out cloth setting the spirit free!"

"Oh, this concept has done so much harm to this country and has weakened our hold on material realities. But this is a misreading of the ancient scriptures. After all, why would the Spirit create this or any other world at all if it had no purpose save a trap? And if it is really so, then one has to agree that it is not some All-wise spirit but an insane mind that created this world. But this is not true. The Upanishads boldly declare that the Spirit chose to enter into these countless worlds after it created them and chose to dwell within the human body." The Master was in a mood to reveal truths unheard.

He continued, adding revelation upon revelation, "Yes, it is the Spirit that has become Matter and then entered into it and these countless worlds through many steps and each of its step is a world in its own right. Now, in return matter is trying to rediscover or become the Spirit and climbs through all the intermediary steps and their worlds whose influence kneads matter. This body itself is built not only by pure matter as you know it but also by an influence from life-worlds and mind-worlds and is now being moulded and prepared under the pressure of the spirit-world."

One trying to grasp the subtlety of the truth asked, "Is that why our thoughts, impulses and feelings have an effect upon the body?"

"Yes, indeed," the Master looked happy. "If our thoughts are ugly and unclean, our feelings narrow and turbulent, our will small and tied to petty gains and selfish aims, then the house of the soul becomes a thing small and dark, with little space or fresh air, with not enough sunlight, like a dingy and dusty corner full of the smoke of desires and passions, full of the fumes of anger and jealousy and hatred."

"I see now, what you meant when you said that men spend a lifetime to build a house of mud but take little care of this bodily house. Perhaps that is why we remain so unhappy even in a palace."

"Yes," the Master's face beamed again. "The joy, the delight one experiences is directly linked to the psychological space of your inner dwelling. If it is small and narrow, full of dust and smoke then one is perpetually restless and unhappy, stifled by the smoke. Naturally, gods do not like to dwell in such an atmosphere. They depart one by one leaving the house at ransom for dark and evil forces that are always waiting."

"And what about the soul?" asked one.

"The soul silently witnesses and endures waiting for nature to be ready as it must one day, or else remains asleep, unable to express its beauty and goodness and light and truth in that stifling atmosphere. Till it too chooses to depart." The Master paused: "This is the inner tragedy to be the world's king but abandoned by one's soul. But men run after worldly success and if they fail they think it is a tragedy though often worldly misfortune is a great blessing."

"A blessing, but how?" asked someone.

"For through it, men can once again turn to their soul for support. When tragedy strikes and the charm of outer things is lost, then we have a chance to awaken to the inner realities."

"But we always thought that success and a rich, comfortable life, free of failure is a gift from God, a reward of good deeds," asked one steeped in traditions.

"That is why I said that this world is an inverse image of Truth and all its values are turned upside down." The Master observed again and plunged into a deep Silence that brooded always in his atmosphere. And as he thus plunged, a hope arose in the hearts of those gathered around him. One voiced it, inversely again "How can this inversion be set right, Master, or is it always meant to be so?"

The Master lifted his compassionate gaze and looking as if far-off to some future dawn awaiting its hour guarded by the folds of darkness softly replied, "We shall leave this for some other time…"

Ways of the Master

The disciples sometimes wondered about the Master's behaviour. He would gather all kinds of people around him even those who seemed worse than ordinary men. One voiced his doubt. The Master smiled as he replied: "Wouldst thou measure the worth of a seed by the thickness of its casing, the height of a man by the size of his shoe, the dimensions of his inner being by the girth of his belly? So too judge not the inner truth of a man by his outer behaviour nor measure his soul's aspiration by his outer virtues. A great light may throw up a great shadow behind it. And a most ordinary looking shell may hide beneath its wings a rare invaluable pearl."

The sceptics wondered why some disciples progressed faster than others. The Master pointed at a rich harvest and answered: "The souls that come to me are like a seed. I am the farmer who ploughs the soil and sows the seeds giving an equal opportunity of the light of sun and the rain of Grace to all. Some seeds however are afraid of the Light and fail to burst open. Other are over eager to draw the sun to themselves and get burnt out. Some, the rare few, trust my hands and the time taken for fruition and do not cling to the dark womb of safety. They are the happiest and the luckiest ones that throw the richest harvest."

"How does one know that the soul has awakened?" asked another. The Master pointed at the early morning sun and observed: "How does one know that the sun has arisen? By a light that illumines our sight driving away the grey phantom shadows of the night; by the song of the birds that greet the dawn. By the rush of a joy that is full of glad peace and a stillness that carries happiness in its bosom. By the silver lining of hope that begins to appear from behind the clouds. By a scattering of the fog and mist and the warmth of a glow within the heart. By the feeling of an urge to grow and an invitation to work and progress. By discovering the love that binds the sky to the earth and all that exists upon it. By seeing the Fire and Light ascend to higher and higher skies. So too with the awakening of the soul one feels a growing peace and joy within the heart, one begins to see hope behind even the darkest appearances, there is birth of faith and aspiration and prayer. A warmth and sweetness and enthusiasm for Godward effort and the urge for progress. Most of all love is born, true love, in the human heart and there is a smile in every circumstance.

Karna, the Fallen Great

The Master had just finished reading the *Karna Parva* (the book of Karna}. The story always carried a touch of sadness at the fall of a hero, an apparent inglorious death, in ways not befitting a hero. After all, he was the eldest Pandava, who knew not his identity until the beginning of the war. He was trained by no less a warrior than Parashuram and, most of all, he was guarded by none other than the Sun-God whose child he was. Generous to a default, Karna's only fault seems to have been standing by Duryodhana's side and, thereby, helping the forces of adharma. But was it not in deference to his friendship and his promise to always be by the side of his friend Duryodhana? So, what was the reason for this strange fate that had punished virtue with a life of such ignominy?

Though Bhisma too met an inglorious death and one that entailed great suffering, both physical and psychological, yet his fall was justified as if there ever was one person who could have stopped this war it was Bhisma. Instead, he chose to stand by his promise given to the throne of Hastinapur even if the dynasty was involved in adharma. The result was a bed of arrows at the hands of his most loved grandchild, who was aided by Shikhandi, the transwoman warrior. But Karna was simply following the law of friendship. Why should he have met such a death? The modern question was swirling in the heads of the disciples. For the men in the ancient times, it was evident that the fate of a man standing by the side of adharma was a long-foregone conclusion. Even if he won for the moment as Shakuni and his scheming nephews did, eventually it was Truth that had the last stroke, *satyameva jayate nanrtam*, it is truth that wins and not falsehood. And Karna was surely standing on the wrong side of history. He stood with his shining armour to defend the indefensible and paid the price with his death. For the ancient mind this was clear. But the disciples were modern minded and demanded equal rights for everybody. They felt that destiny and God were unfair towards Karna.

The Master had seen this question brewing up in their mind. As was his way to address things often from examples of nature he pointed his fingers towards a storm that was brewing up in the far end of the sky.

"Look, how the storm is covering the sky and dimming the sun."

The disciples nodded at the very evident phenomenon which they had often witnessed during this part of the year. But herein lay the difference between them and the Master. The Master saw in it a lesson of life that the wisdom hidden within Nature tries to reveal to us. But the average person saw only a natural phenomenon that can be explained by the laws of physics.

"Do you see how the sandstorm overpowers the mighty sun, even if temporarily? Of course, the sun remains untouched by it but its rays are unable to reach the earth in their fullness."

The disciples had begun to notice the drift.

"So too", the Master continued, "even the strong and the wise may be clouded by the storms of passion and ambition, lust and greed which may block their intelligence and prevent it from making the right choice."

The disciples were all ears. The Master continued, "This is what happened to Karna. Though high of birth and mighty in deeds, his stainless soul was clouded by his strong ambition to prove himself to the world that he is the greatest by defeating Arjuna. The chariot of his life began to be driven by ambition and had to meet its nemesis one day. He swerved away from Dharma as invariably ambition leads one away from the straight path of the soul. The result was that his journey ended abruptly, crashed as it were in the quagmire of ambition. Arjuna's last blow, the fatal arrow only completed the work, hastening him back to his beautiful soul, in a way putting him on the right track preventing him from bearing the burden of adharma even more. In fact, Bhisma stopping him from the battle, Sri Krishna's offer to him to switch over to the Pandava side was not only a ploy to ensure the safety of Arjuna who was an instrument of God in the battlefield of Kurukshetra, but also to prevent Karna from bearing the tremendous burden of defending the champions of evil and thereby himself becoming a party to it."

Then pausing for a moment in deep reflection, the Master added, "Karna was saved by his own death. He was destined to die because of his choice. Yet had he died normally it would have been a miserable death, a humiliating defeat. He had to die because he was standing between the Lord's Will and haughty, ambition-driven, lust-laden Kuru clan typified in the likes of Duryodhana. By dying the way he did, at least his name was saved. It was an act of Compassion of Vasudeva, the indwelling Universal Divine, the lover of all mankind and the friend of all creatures."

"But still wasn't his choice based on his feeling of gratitude towards his friend Duryodhana?" asked one.

The Master gently smiled and looking towards the sky where the storm had begun to clear up, he asked the disciple if he really thought so? The disciple stood perplexed as the Master answered.

"Would it not have been a better expression of gratitude if he abstained from the unjust war and thereby, possibly prevented it? Should he have not counseled his friend that this war would not only do no good for him but bring ignominy and gloom? He did not, even though being the child of the sun-god he well understood which side stands for the truth and the right. He did not because he saw in the war his one chance of proving himself in a mortal combat with Arjuna that he is the greatest between the two. If he was feeling gratitude for having been given a kingdom by Duryodhana to satisfy his ambition, an even better choice would have been to return back the kingdom and unburden himself rather than take his side in an unjust war. Have you not heard the story of Esau and Jacob wherein Esau loses his birthright bartering it for a pot of porridge to appease his hunger? It is just the same story wherein one loses one's soul, the birthright, for the sake of satisfying one's ambition by joining the forces of evil. "

"But was not life unfair to him, his being cast away by his mother at the very moment of his birth?" One in the group observed in a half-hearted voice knowing that this had little to do with Karna's eventual fate.

"Yes indeed, if you look at life from a human perspective of fair dealings, life was surely unfair to Karna. But was it not unfair to the Pandava brothers even more? And what did the prince Duryodhana do with whom life was more than fair? So you see, the game of life is not fair and unfair but about the challenges through which we grow by making our choices. The greater the possibility, the more challenging is the dice. The greater grow wiser and stronger by the stroke. The weak succumb to their desires and choose unwisely. That in short sums up the story of Karna."

The Master paused as the storm had begun to calm and the sun shone more clearly in the eastern sky.

The rays had begun to dance again upon earth and one looking at the rays imagined Karna's soul uplifted towards the sun through his death shedding his burdened cloak upon earth.

Adhikara Bheda

The Master shared many secrets of living. One of them was to be as a flower shedding its fragrance for all while drawing all its needs from the soil and the sun. "Be like a flower," he would say, "open, frank, generous, equal and kind." Or else sometimes he would teach the disciples to emulate the best quality in each creature, the faithfulness of a dog, the sensitivity of a cat, the swiftness of a deer, quiet strength of a lion, the purity and discernment of the swan, the concentration of the kingfisher and the perseverance of the crow. He would also teach through material nature saying that the language of God is everywhere. This was the Veda written through material objects as letters. Be as the mountain, firm and high, carrying the aspiration of earth heavenwards. Or be as the star, stationed high yet guiding man and showing him the direction and the path through stormy seas. Or else, be as the river, he would say, that knows its origin and the goal and rushes towards it circuiting through every obstacle on its way.

The disciples would thus learn through images of earth something which could be reflected in their own human nature. One day the subject turned towards how to know one's own true nature. "Each one of us has something divine in us", he said, "and it is our business to cultivate it and live according to it." But he cautioned that there is also in each one something covering this true divine nature, diverting us from our true divine impulse into lanes and by-lanes that were never meant for us, thereby, creating much confusion within the individual and the society. In the course of such a conversation, the subject turned to *Adhikara bheda* or the distinction that needs to be made between different aspirants and seekers. It is for this reason that the Master was not in favour of a standardized practice to be given to one and all who came to him. To some he would ask to meditate, while to others he would assign a work, some he would ask to till the fields while to others he would ask to work in the kitchen. Yet others were asked to read and write or paint and draw while some others were even sent for a vigorous training in physical education. Each, therefore, had his own unique path through which one moved towards his self-development towards a higher spiritual evolution which he foresaw as the imminent future of man. The disciples unable to understand asked him as to why it was so. The Master replied that the ancient Indian Society was built upon this profound understanding that each individual is at a different stage of evolution and has his or her own unique calling. Not all can or should do the same thing, he stated, which was, of course, an obvious fact. It is this that was known as *Adhikara Bheda*, which was lost to the modern mind.

And then to illustrate he went on to narrate the Eklavya story from the Mahabharata.

"Do you remember how Dronacharya asked Eklavya his right-hand thumb as *guru dakshina*?"

"Oh yes Master," one remarked, expressing his dismay at the injustice meted out to the apprentice by Dronacharya.

The Master smiled and explained the story thus.

"You see Dronacharya was the teacher appointed for the royal princes. In those days, the task of war was left to the Kshatriyas to avoid a large-scale conflict. It was the Kshatriya alone who could learn the various skills of war which sometimes involved high technology skills as were available in those times. It would be a disaster if this high technology of wielding powerful and devastating weapons, some of which were as good as our modern nuclear arms, was offered to all. Hence it was not made available to all and sundry, even if one could pay a fee. Hence, Eklavya was denied the right to study under Dronacharya. But you see he could have tried to find another teacher as Karna did. But instead, he chose to steal knowledge in hiding."

"Master we can understand that. But still what was the need to take away his thumb and incapacitate him from using what he had already learned?" One among them asked.

"Don't you know how the circumstances unfolded? There was a hound that was accompanying the entourage of Dronacharya. The dog smelt that someone was hiding and began to bark. Seeing him thus and worried about his identity and stealth being disclosed Eklavya shot a volley of arrows stuffing the mouth of the dog. What do you think of such a warrior if the actions of a man were a judge of things?" the Master asked.

One of them answered, "It was quite a cruel thing to do."

"Yes, a cruel misuse of one's prowess. No wonder Dronacharya felt it wiser to stay the errant warrior then and there, lest he became a menace for mankind."

Then returning to the disciples, the Master remarked, "You see a Master is like a wide river that carries whatever enters in his flow. But then not all are ready to bear the shock of the journey. Hence some are accepted while others are not. People who do not understand the ways of a Master think he is being partial. But, in fact, even his rejections are simply postponements and are a sign of compassion and grace. The Master waits and prepares the disciple, even though, he is not yet part of the mighty spiritual current until they are ready and grow strong enough to bear the force and the flood of the Divine Force and the love and the intensity of His Light."

The Second Coming

The atmosphere was solemn but not heavy. There was a lightness and a Light that one always felt in the Master's presence. But the solemnness of the occasion was because of the Master's illness. The Master had not been well for the last couple of weeks, and now he seemed to be withdrawing, suddenly, as sun assumes the crimson golden hue of dawn just before setting in the western seas, the Master came back to his full outer awareness and smiled at the grave faces that had gathered around him in the dusk.

The Master broke the silence, or rather enriched it by his sweet and liquid voice that always seemed to come from some far-off world, "What makes your faces so grave?" One among them answered with a rather low voice, "Your illness, Master and the fear we all share that you may leave us."

There was a pause as between the destruction and creation of worlds. The Master seemed to have lapsed again. But he came out of his trance soon enough. Slowly, he responded to the disciple's anxiety,

"But where am I leaving you? Do you think I am this body?" The Master pinched his flesh at places while saying so, and continued, "None of us are mere physical bodies. Only you are not conscious of it whereas I am fully conscious of my deathless Self and the many births before. And the deathless Self is immortal. It does not die."

The conversation had started. Another continued the thread, "You are God, aren't you?"

The Master paused a while, "Yes, but it is also true of all of you, only you do not know it.

The disciple asked, "But you are God in a special sense, an avatara, the Supreme incarnated in a material body. You are not like us struggling from below upwards."

The Master replied, "Yes, but so were Krishna, Christ and Buddha avatara, conscious of their Godhead. Do you think an avatara is not subject to the laws of the earth when he takes up a human body?

And the disciple continued, "We thought so, an avatara is free from the laws that govern us mortals."

The Master said with a great force in his words, "None of us is a mortal. Bondage is an illusion. Death is an illusion. There is none bound, none dies. Have you forgotten the great injunction of Sri Krishna, 'It is only forms that perish, the soul is immortal.' Did he not also say 'There was never a time when I or these kings were not there, nor when they will not'?"

The Master looked at them with a powerful gaze. Then as the glow softened, he continued, "Do you think that Sri Krishna, Christ, Buddha are dead and gone? Have I not told you of my own encounters with them, especially with Sri Krishna, the eternal friend and lover of all mankind in whose arms of ecstasy I spent days and weeks? How could I if he were no more? In fact, an avatara never leaves the earth. He comes for the earth and stays here as a permanent part of the earth consciousness so that all who rightly strive may be helped by him and arrive."

The disciples looked puzzled. Of course, they had read all this but somehow seemed to forget it. How foolish of them to believe that the Master could ever leave them. The Master as if read their thoughts, "How could I ever leave you? No, I will be present upon earth till the work for which I have come is done. Only you would not see me with your physical senses."

"That makes a great difference to us," one of them pleadingly complained.

But the Master reassured, "But my help will always be available just as ever. Those who have a subtle vision can even see me."

"But your physical presence…"

The Master revealed, "Do you think the Divine takes up a physical body only to guide a few handfuls of people who are near him? He can and does do that even without assuming a physical body. The experience of many devotees and saints testifies this."

The disciple insisted, "But still your physical presence makes a great difference."

The Master looked at them with great compassion, "It does serve as a concrete example but one cannot profit by physical nearness alone. The Master is a doorway to help you discover the Divine Master within you. One too often forgets that simply because the Master is physically available and readily accessible. In fact, the help of the Master is not so much by the words he utters and the letters to which he replies, for these can be readily misinterpreted. His real help reaches out as a silent but powerful influence, to all who are receptive and open. And this help and influence are not dependent upon the physical Presence, though men find it easier to open to someone who is concretely visible in flesh and blood. But that is man's limitation, not the Master's. He acts without hands and feet, speaks without the tongue and influences us even while he is bodiless. Indeed, that is the Master's mode of action even while he is in the body."

A little puzzled one with logical reasoning asked, "Then why does God take up a body at all if He can guide men and the world without taking up a human body? And if He does, why does he seem to suffer and even fall ill and die like ordinary mortals?"

"Oh, that is another matter. It is not about guidance but about doing something with physical matter or the earth substance. The Divine takes up a human body as a field of action directly upon Matter and the physical conditions of the earth. Now also He acts but from behind, through many layers that clothe and conceal Him. Therefore, the work upon earth seems so abominably slow, difficult, and painful. But by taking up a physical body, the Divine can bring the very physical substance and earth-nature directly in contact with the Divine Forces from another plane of a higher consciousness. That helps the earth and embodied beings progress as a whole, collectively and not just a few special chosen men. It makes the earth cover as if in one giant leap of a few decades or centuries what it would otherwise take millenniums to realise."

"Oh yes, we can see that; how your coming revolutionized the entire face of the earth. The very atmosphere has changed," a disciple observed, but then added, as if with a tinge of doubt, "that is why we cannot understand your illness all the more. We have seen and experienced your powerful Presence and its Influence several times ourselves and in the world. To say the least, we have seen you cure such intractable illnesses in others. So why or how could you not cure yourself?"

The Master spoke as if enigmatically, "Maybe I could cure myself but would not. Maybe I wish to experience all that human beings experience including illness and death so that I can change their law. How could I do it unless I experience it? How can I change the law unless I fully know it? It is easy to pass beyond the law and remain above it, it is also easy enough to superimpose the law of one plane upon another, but it is extremely difficult to change the law of one plane into another."

The disciples looked quizzically at each other, "What does that mean? We do not quite grasp that."

The Master explained, "It is easy, for example, for a yogi to keep his body alive and healthy for a long period by superimposing upon it the vital force, or else, to simply rise above his illness and be free within of all reactions. That is how miracles ordinarily work. But when you want to change the material laws, then that is another thing altogether. In the previous two, you rise above them or else momentarily suspend or hold them in abeyance for whatever period you wish to with constant superior control. It is like policing. The presence of the police controls the thief so long as they are vigilant but it does not change a thief or criminal. For that, you have to enter into the criminal's mind and consciousness and know it by a kind of identification, of course without losing your own identity. It is a deliberate process. You do this not out of any weakness but out of strength, to understand how they think and operate, what is their origin due to. And all this so as to transform them. That is transforming the law."

"But won't that upset the balance," one reflectively demurred.

"It would do so only if the law were such at the origin and fixed for all times. But that is not the case. Earth and physical life have become what it is not because it is radically and incurably false in their origin. Quite the contrary, their origin, as indeed the origin of all things is Truth and Consciousness and Bliss. But, in the course of time, it has become almost its opposite." The Master paused, reflectively as if the whole course of earth's history stood before him in one panoramic flash.

"But why did this fall from Glory come out?" someone steeped in tradition asked seizing upon the pause.

The Master once again turned towards them, "Oh! haven't you read, I have written all that in great detail elsewhere." Some of them could notice the touch of gentle irony in the Master's words, haven't you read, as if observing human complacency. For these were his ways, gentle and subtle yet unfailing in pointing us the road of Light.

He continued, "Nevertheless, the fact that everything has issued forth from the Divine and contains His Presence within it, therefore, everything is not only potentially Divine but also destined to become more and more so through an evolutionary process. Matter too, despite all its inertness and unconsciousness is divine in its origin and in human beings, it has already reached a point wherein it can be divinized. The Divine descends upon earth and takes a physical body to redeem matter and liberate the godhead concealed in it."

With a flash of intuition, one observed, "Oh! like that story of Ahalya who becomes stone due to a curse and then turns into a goddess by the grace of Lord Rama's touch."

Another ventured to ask, "Is that the reason why Divine comes again and again upon earth and takes up a physical body? Is this the second coming spoken of in the great traditions of Hinduism, Christianity and Buddhism?"

The Master answered, "The second coming is not a religious event. It is not the resurrection of a certain creed or Church or a theology nor is it to save a particular religious group. The second coming is precisely this—the complete victory of the Divine upon earth, this reign of Truth and Light in this world, the Divine advent in all His Glory and not as He is presently concealed in the thick cloak of a human body. The second coming is about the coming of the Divine in a divinized body, a body befitting the Mighty Presence."

The disciples were awestruck. How vast was the Master's vision and how small and narrow their ignorant beliefs? After a long silence one asked, "So you will come again."

The Master nodded in assent and added, "Yes, in a divinized body. For only such a body can truly fuse and express all the diverse aspects of the One Divine who comes as Krishna, Christ, Buddha and the rest."

One pleaded, "How will we recognize you?"

And the Master said, "That is one reason why I must depart. So that you open your inner eyes and find me there. For they who have this inner vision will always find me for they know me as the Supreme Godhead who has assumed this form. For them, the form is the door to the world of Light and Truth. But those who see the form alone and know Me only by my external personality will try to make a cult and a religion or an intellectual creed and dogma and philosophy out of it. That is what man has always done so far with the Divine. But with the second coming all this will cease, for the Divine will no more be hidden by the form nor will He need the imperfect figures of idea and philosophy or religion to express Himself in this world. The second coming is the great return, the return of the Divine as the revealed and not a concealed sovereign and King upon earth. That will also be the establishment of the Divine Kingdom here, the dream of all religions and the hope of mankind."

The Master's words fell silent in the fast-gathering night. But a hope stole in the heart of the earth and the Light of a New Dawn waited in the Eastern sky for the appropriate hour.

Books by BluOne Ink

Kali

Sri Aurobindo & the Literary Renaissance of India | Pariksith Singh
ISBN: 9788194954781 | ₹995

Sri Aurobindo and Philosophy | Pariksith Singh
ISBN: 9789392209017 | ₹995

Somewhere Among the Stars | Adi Varuni
ISBN: 9789392209215 | ₹395

The Eternal Feminine | Dr Alok Pandey
ISBN: 9788194954774 | ₹699

Integral Education | Partho
ISBN: 9788194954705 | ₹499

Hindutva: Origin, Evolution and Future | Aravindan Neelakandan
ISBN: 9789392209062 | ₹995

BluPrint

Identity's Last Secret | Makarand R. Paranjape
ISBN: 9788194954798 | ₹1495

Swayam Se Parichay (in Hindi) | Pariksith Singh
ISBN: 9789392209185 | ₹195

Chhutti Ke Din (bilingual in Hindi and Rajasthani) | Pariksith Singh
ISBN: 9789392209024 | ₹699

Anjali Geetan Ri (in Rajasthani) | Ikram Rajasthani
ISBN: 9789392209277 | ₹250

Jana Awjanar Majhe (in Bengali) | Bimal Chakravartty
ISBN: 9789392209277 | ₹250

The Eternal Gene and Other Tales of Malaise | Ankush Sam Thorpe
ISBN: 9789392209147 | ₹495

Swayam Ka Ghupaithiya (bilingual in Hindi and Rajasthani) |
Pariksith Singh
ISBN: 9789392209192 | ₹699

All Stray Dogs Go to Heaven | Krishna Candeth
ISBN: 9789392209086 | ₹695

Occam
Confidence Cures | Lt. Gen. S.B. Sehajpal and Mrs Kiran Sehajpal
ISBN: 9789392209260 | ₹495

War Despatches 1971 | Brig. B.S. Mehta (Ed.)
ISBN: 9789392209123 | ₹899

March to Justice | Navdeep Singh and Frank Rosenblatt
ISBN: 9788194954712 | ₹995

The Fighting Fourth | Brig. Jasbir Singh, SM
ISBN: 9788194954750 | ₹699

Once Upon a Time in RIMC | Brig. Jasbir Singh, SM
ISBN: 9788194954729 | ₹250

Design: A Business Case | Brigitte Borja de Mozota and
Steinar Valade-Amland
ISBN: 9788194954743 | ₹795

MRA Made Simple: Seriously? | Pariksith Singh, MD and
Lynda Dilts-Benson
ISBN: 9781954261006 | $29.99

Compliance Made Simple: Seriously? | Pariksith Singh, MD and
Lynda Dilts-Benson
ISBN: 9781954261013 | $55.99

Snakes in the Ganga: Breaking India 2.0 | Rajiv Malhotra and
Vijaya Viswanathan
ISBN: 9789392209093 | ₹895

Life of an Industani: Six Degrees of Separation | Shiv Kunal Verma
ISBN: 9789392209154 | ₹995

Grit to Glory | Brig. B.S. Mehta
ISBN: 9789392209291 | ₹895

The Battle for IITs: A Defense of Meritocracy | Rajiv Malhotra and Vijaya Viswanathan
ISBN: 9789392209314 | ₹250

Varna, Jati, Caste: A Primer on Indian Social Structures | Rajiv Malhotra and Vijaya Viswanathan
ISBN: 9789392209345 | ₹250

The Power of Future Machines: Essays on Artificial Intelligence | Rajiv Malhotra, T.N. Sudarshan and Manogna Sastry (Eds)
ISBN: 9789392209338 | ₹750

Of Newtons and Apples: Insights into 50 Great Minds in Human History | Dr Abhishek Kumar
ISBN: 9789392209246 | ₹350

Our Forthcoming Titles

Seeing with Hands | Jinan K.B.
ISBN: 9789392209000

The Quest: A Search for the Undefined through Defined Forms | Aparajita Barai
ISBN: 9789392209239

www.ingramcontent.com/pod-product-compliance
Lightning Source LLC
LaVergne TN
LVHW041850070526
838199LV00045BB/1520